Broken

Just to be made new

by
Hugh J. Harmon

Kingdom Book & Gift LLP
Columbia, South Carolina

Hugh J Harmon

Broken

Just to be made new

Published by **KINGDOM BOOK & GIFT LLP**
P.O. Box 291975
Columbia, SC 29229
803-736-2472
www.kingdombookandgift.com

ISBN 978-0-6151-6321-5
Library of Congress
Printed in the United States of America

I dedicate this book to Auntie Arlette, in the face of breaking you have held your head up, and you have held onto the faith. Don't weary in well doing: for in due season you shall reap, if you faint not. Trust God, *for they that trust in the Lord shall be as mount Zion, which cannot be removed, but abideth forever* (Psa. 125:1)

Contents

Preface

As I sat down to write this book, I was led to address an issue that has grown dear to my heart, and I believe has been an issue that many believers have wrestled with over the life of their walk with Christ. It is the issue of feeling that despite ones new allegiance to Christ, the vicissitudes of life still seem to be leveled at us almost as steadily, and with even greater affect than when we were unsaved. This is what I like to call the "brokenness factor". The concern isn't that we are facing trials and tribulation; that is to be expected. What makes this issue a critical one is the response that we have to the trouble that we face. The onset of trouble can soon become despair especially for one who is newly converted to Christ only to be faced with direct attack from the enemy of our souls. The thought life of this person can turn from one aflame with hope for tomorrow to one who feels disappointed and forsaken by a God that they just came to know. Too often than necessary this can be the first sign of a life spiraling down into self-inflicted brokenness.

Brokenness is the unsung principle of God's dealing with his people. Some theologians may even vigorously deny its relevance as a means by which God works out transformation in our lives. It is a place in God that can be a challenge to our long standing view of God and his graciousness. The key to clarity in our understanding in this area of God's redemptive plan is for us not to mix up man's wounding with God's breaking. We wound each other on a regular basis, in word and in action, and with no significant purpose beyond inflicting pain. We leave scars of resentment and distrust in an effort to exact revenge for some perceived wrong done toward us. Sometimes we wound others simply as a measure of evening what we see as an unfair advantage someone has over us in the playing field of life. These scars in turn are very hard to erase. The people that we hurt in an effort to make ourselves feel better, on occasion bare these hurt feelings and bruised egos for years after the fact. But brokenness in the hands of God is not an act of deliberate disfiguring or harm, but rather it is an act of deconstructing our self-knowledge and our addiction to independence, so that we may be brought to a place of awareness of our complete dependence upon Him.

Broken, just to be made new, the idea is a difficult one to swallow. The thought that a great and gracious God has need of breaking us in order that we might be made suitable for kingdom service in the long run is one that many Christians find hard to reconcile. Most of the time we are taught to believe that God's aim is to shield us from all hurt and harm, and he would never be the agent of hurt in our lives. And this still stands true. But in our season of brokenness, hurt is a very real feeling that we will experience. Nevertheless, hurt being as it may, is not the intended sensation that we must take away from the experience. But rather, should be a driving force to push us into our place of transformation.

Today, as we examine the nature of mankind, especially the men and women of this world that stand with no alliance to a Redeeming Savior, a quick self-examination will soon lay bare to the fact that unsaved mankind is a depraved being. Without salvation through the shed blood of Jesus Christ, we would do just about anything that we could set our minds to do and our hearts to desire. This shows that man's fallen nature, driven by self-gratification, is rooted in sin, and that nature, must be remade. Not only must it be remade, but it must also be renewed. Hence, before remaking can occur something must be unmade or taken apart.

Every man and woman born into this world is born unbroken, and we all need to be broken. It is quite a harsh thing to say but it has to be repeated because it is the truth. Every man and woman born into this world is born unbroken, and we all need to be broken. And brokenness is such a divisive and deeply rooted condition that even after surrendering to a life in Christ, we can unconsciously bring our broken mindset into our new walk with Him. Salvation in the pure sense of the experience of being born again is a finished work. It is a work that renders us new, *old things are passed away and all things become new*. However, what sense is it if we have a new life to work with but we are working with the same old mind. This is the situation with many believers who are struggling in their salvation. They have been able, in their minds, to jointly possess faith in Jesus Christ as their Savior and Lord, while at the same time having a distorted view of their relevancy within the plan of God. It makes no sense knowing God but yet still believing that he will never know you, or even more damaging believing that he doesn't want to know you. New life in Christ is only relevant to the man or woman that can recognize the new life and take the steps to model it for the rest of the world that still has not received Him.

As you delve into this adventure of sorts, Broken, just to be made new, I trust and pray that you will see a familiar and similar place to that which you may be going through. And in seeing that place in this text, may you follow the path in these pages and in following fully experience the breaking that is of Christ. Then and only then will you be ready to be of real service to God. This book could never stand alone as a device to deal with the wiles of the enemy and with the powerful pull of our own self-will. This is why I would encourage you to make the Bible, the center of your life when it comes to your search for answers. **Broken, just to be made new** can only accompany the Word and give the human perspective of one who has been where you are. The Word is *a lamp to our feet and a light unto our path*, even if that path currently is strewn with pain. May this book inspire you to get closer to God and in turn drive you to get into His Word that you may be able to stand on the promises that He has made to us all before, during and after the breaking.

As a seed must be broken before it can bring forth fruit, so too must the indispensable act of our breaking take place that we may be fruitful, and the glory of God can be fully manifested in our lives.

1.

Overcoming the feeling of failure

And the Lord turned, and looked upon Peter. And Peter remembered the word of the Lord, how he had said unto him, Before the cock crow, thou shalt deny me thrice.
And Peter went out, and wept bitterly.

Luke 22:61,62

He was broken.

I could imagine how Peter must have felt. The sting of guilt must have shot up his spine. His esteem was definitively shot. The boldness that marked his persona was dealt a crushing blow. Here stood, one of Jesus' boldest and in some respects, clearly his most forthright follower caught in a moment of great compromise. Despite the fact that Jesus had foretold of his impending misstep it still didn't take away from the feeling of great failure he now felt. He was broken. The text says that Peter did the deed and almost immediately afterward comes face to face with the subject of his denial, Jesus. It wasn't enough that he had done what he had sworn that he wouldn't do but that he did it and was caught. He was broken. Jesus had become the center of his life. Peter had left family, friends and even his fishing (his way of livelihood) to follow Jesus. Now he found himself in the place of denial of the one whom he had admittedly grown to love. Peter was broken. He was in a place of absolute disappointment in self, and the feeling of failure was inevitable.

Life has a way of sometimes handing us outcomes that fall way short of our expectations. Disappointment can many times be the daunting companion of great expectations. But think about it, how could we develop a mindset of great expectation if we never have to deal with the possibility of falling short? The frequency with which we encounter short falls can cause us to adopt an attitude of failure. This attitude of failure in turn could breed a sentiment of brokenness. Have you ever felt broken? Are there times when you have felt that every dream or aspiration toward which you have pressed has resulted in a path to nowhere? Maybe you've found yourself in a long-term financial rut. You may feel yourself stuck in a career with no room for advancement. If you're still in school or struggling to complete school maybe academically you feel as if you should be further along in your education than you currently are. The feeling of failure is the constant traveling partner of those who dream big but have very little resources to actively pursue their dreams. If you dream big either about your life, your relationships or your possessions the possibility of encountering more disappointment than success is real. That is the risk we take when we are dreamers. And as dreamers, many times disappointment at an unrealized dream can be an indication of one being, as it were, broken.

Accepting the entitlement of brokenness can be one of the most difficult decisions for one to make in life. The difficulty does not lie in us fully grasping reality but rather lies in us resting in the understanding that we are less than perfect. If I say that I am broken, I am admitting that there

9

is something about me that is less than complete. To be broken would be an acceptance that I am less than whole. It is difficult for us to wrap our minds around the idea of being less than whole, but yet still broken may be the best place for us to be.

Several hundreds of years prior to the troubling experience of Peter, another man with just as much boldness and empowered with great potential also found himself broken. Peter was a poor ex-fisherman who once plowed the banks of the Jordan, who had decided to give up all that he knew and essentially had, to follow the stepson of a poor carpenter. In a bout of fear, he did what he thought he was incapable of doing and he was left broken. Jacob, the son of the great patriarch Isaac also had a bout with brokenness despite his status as an heir to the great promise and being a wealthy man to boot. Jacob had a son. It was the son that he favored above all his other children because he was the child of his old age. Joseph too had his season of brokenness. Moses the great deliverer of the ancient Hebrew people from their place of bondage in Egypt also went through the experience of being broken. The list of great men and women of mark that have been broken at some time in their lives can go on and on. The stories are divergent and the characters vary in background but there is one striking similarity. These men and women all accepted and answered in the affirmative to the request, "Can you stand to be broken, just to be made new?"

In the eyes of men, being broken is a sign of weakness. In the eyes of God, however, it is a sign of impending greatness. Broken men and women often become the refuse of society. They become institutionalized. They are made captives left to relish in the sense of failure, seldom given any devices by which they could reform themselves. Rather they are given tools by which they could mask the scars, the pain and the faults. But to be broken in the presence of God is to be placed in a position where everything that isn't right could be made whole. The broken pieces of our lives are ever available for disposal on the refuse heap of this world, or for placement in the hands of God. You choose the place where your broken pieces will end up.

What does it mean to be broken? Is broken merely a financial or monetary state? Is it just an indication of one's lack of material goods? We could get caught up with the term "being broke." But I believe to be broken supersedes even just the lack of things because there are many wealthy men and women in this world who would fall into the category of being broken. Are all the broken people incarcerated or hospitalized? Are they all deficient medically, physically or mentally? Or is it something less obvious? I would have to say something less obvious. The type of brokenness that I am talking about is the type that men mask in over commitment to work, women mask in over indulgence in shopping, and children mask in over aggression. It is the type of broken that we all have been able to artfully cope with from time to time, the type of broken that only you and God know about. It can hinder you from all that life has in store for you. The brokenness that is distinguished only by God is the breaking that happens deep down in our hearts.

To be broken is to be dismembered or crushed in the spirit. It is to be in a place in life where you are aware of the fact that everything about you is not totally intact. To be broken is to be the candidate of disconnect-possessing many unhinged parts. Brokenness, in and of itself, has always carried with it a negative connotation. However, it is a condition that can possess great positive value. Each and every one of the great men and women of biblical history experienced their greatest triumphs after the experience of what appeared to be utter brokenness. It wasn't because of their great ability to reinvent themselves or their commitment to life changing resolutions but rather it was as a result of a faithful God who sought opportunities to redeem

11

those dear to his heart, especially at their weakest moment. The Bible says that when we are weak, He is made strong. It says that His strength is made perfect in our weakness. Brokenness teaches us that when we fully accept our weakness, then God can fully strengthen us, because His strength is complete, unlike ours. We are individual members of the body of Christ, our strength is fully accomplished only when we unify with other members of the body in faith. God takes the unified strength of his members and He deposits it in us and this is how our brokenness is fixed.

How does one come into this condition of brokenness? In the body of believers or outside of the body of believers, brokenness is a reality of life. I like to use the analogy of a jigsaw puzzle or a lego construction set of a young child. In both forms of entertainment the fun is in putting the pieces together, watching the process of the construction and the assembly. The finished product of a completed puzzle or a lego creation may bring joyous satisfaction but the child soon loses interest in what they have made and will often disassemble or deconstruct this apparatus just to once again experience the thrill of the build. Puzzles and lego sets are made for assembly, disassembly and reassembly. Our lives are scripted in certain ways so as to lead to the inevitable cycle of assembly, disassembly and reconstruction. This cycle continues to happen in our lives until we resemble the perfection that God promised we would, if we believed in Him, and trusted His word and judgments.

Given that simple analogy of our life experiences mirroring that of the exploratory play of an ambivalent child, one can see that brokenness is unavoidable. However, when does it really make an entrance into our lives? The onset of brokenness varies with ones station in life. For many fathers brokenness comes in the area of the ability to perform the duties of fatherhood. The duties of protection, provision and preservation of family are areas in which many men crumble

at the first sight of challenge and opposition. For many
mothers the thing that accelerates the breaking is rooted in
the family also. When a woman begins to believe that she is
doing it all alone, or when she feels that she is
unappreciated for what she does to keep the family together
we soon see the initiation of a break. Brokenness is not a
condition that is limited to married couples. It can be more
of a thorn in the side of singles. The single male can be
broken just from the mere fact of separation anxiety. He has
lived for a major fraction of his life, given normal
circumstances, under the care of a matriarchal figure. Then
comes the season of transition to adulthood. Men many
times have to be thrust out of the nest of their parent's
homes and out of the reach of the net of their support, into a
life of self-determination and independence. This transition
can be painful for some, and more often than not leads to
another episode of brokenness. Single females although
more eager to escape the confines of the parental nest
encounter their initial brokenness in quite a different
fashion. The urge to have a family of their own, bear
children of their own, nurture offspring and organize a home,
which are all natural tendencies for a female raised
according to conventional female custom, overwhelms the
daunting experience of independence and self-determination.
However, these tendencies can be hindered by the need to
establish a career, and to do the things that contemporary
society says is more acceptable for the twenty-first century
woman. This leads to another episode of brokenness.
Children too can experience brokenness. When they get to a
level of understanding that with advancing age come greater
responsibility and expectations. The burgeoning
responsibility of the developing child coupled with an ever
rising bar of expectation that many times they cannot see
themselves fulfilling, leads to brokenness.

Brokenness can also be a provoked condition. It may
be outside of natural biological development or socio-
economic circumstance. Brokenness may be as a result of a

violation of trust. We can be violently thrown into the area of brokenness. Our brokenness may be as a result of retribution against us for some past wrong.

One thing about brokenness that sets it apart from most other conditions of its nature is that denial of its existence does not devalue its reality. We may deny that we are broken but we can't make it go away because of that denial. Something must be done proactively to deal with it and to get us through the phase of mending.

Notes on "Overcoming the feeling of failure"
1. *What is the definition of failure?*
    Failure is defined as falling short of, being deficient in, nonperformance, deterioration, or bankruptcy. A failure is defined as an unsuccessful person. Failure can many times be the result of ones perspective. If you were to ever fall and just lay there as you look up it always looks as though you have been setback, and it feels as though you are a loser. However falling is not tantamount to failing. It is just a temporary feeling of lost momentum that can be overcome by simply getting up.

2. *What are the causes of failure?*
    Failure may come as a result of walking contrary to God's will. It can be as a result of disobedience. Failure can be simply due to sin, or the deprivation of good. Not only sinners fail but also Christians can fail too. Inconsistency in prayer, your degree of unbelief (i.e. lack of faith) and not counting the cost of the faith can all lead to failure.

3. *What are your options when you feel the onset of the mindset of failure?*
    The key to dealing with this feeling of failure is to remember that it is essentially a feeling. Life can sometimes seem to be a mixed bag of feelings. Our emotions can many times leave us in a quandary, making rash decisions and opting for permanent solutions to temporary inconveniences. Failure is just one of the many feelings that we may encounter in life being subject to a fallen world. Feeling failure comes with the territory, but it shouldn't be the dominating sensation of our lives. Feeling is defined as an unreasoned conviction. This suggests that feelings are seldom thought out but are assigned firm belief. Feelings are too fickle a sensation for one to

Broken, *just to be made new*

direct ones life by. Give the feeling of failure its due time but keep in mind that *this too shall past.*

2.

Becoming Undone

Marsha rose early that Monday morning. She was excited about the day that lay ahead. She was determined that particular day to change the way others thought of her. It was the first day back from the Christmas recess and Marsha had gotten all that she had dreamed she would have gotten in the way of gifts that year. She had gotten three new outfits including shoes. Her first semester at John F. Kennedy Middle School had been horrible. She seemed to be able to do nothing right. In her own estimation she was an outcast who had no friends and she was the brunt of all the jokes. She also felt that she had gotten to the core of why she wasn't accepted by her peers. She felt that it all stemmed from her less than stellar wardrobe. Marsha's clothes downright "sucked"! Academically she was on the top of her class. Athletically she outran, out jumped and out threw all comers in her peer group. It must have been due to her apparent poor taste in clothing. So Marsha had launched on a campaign to redeem her appearance and reputation for having wardrobe mishaps. It obviously had worked. Whenever a relative had asked her what she had wanted for Christmas she had said that she preferred clothes. She was also very specific as to the store and the styles that suited her fancy.

Marsha carefully dressed, she worked out every unattractive crease that she could find in the mirror as she modeled outfit number one. She had already planned out how she was going to coordinate each top with the matching bottom, and even how she might diversify when necessary to make this good trend last. Finally, she made her choice and shot out the door. She got to school at exactly the right time, when all her classmates were disembarking the school bus. And she was going to walk by slowly so that they could "eat their hearts out!"

The initial reaction was as expected. There was a moment of brief silence. From her periphery she could see both the girls and guys staring at her. She fixed her swagger just to let them know that she knew she was looking good. She turned her head to wave at her adoring fans. But then what happened next was a lot less expected. She walked just a tad bit to close to the wire fence that separated the playground from the schoolyard. Her new sweater got snagged in a loosely protruding wire unbeknownst to Marsha. As she marched on in deep pride Marsha noticed that her sweater started to get tighter and tighter around her upper chest as it started to become undone at the hem. But even more troubling was the rising din of laughter, snickering and giggling that seemed to follow her into the building. Her great day was turning into a bad one quickly. Not only was her sweater becoming undone but also what little dignity she had was undone. Marsha was broken.

Broken in the face of derision, this was what marked Marsha's experience. Our lives can become undone as easily as a snagged sweater. Our circumstances maybe as simple

17

as that described in Marsha's first day back to school or as complex as the quandary that Jacob got himself into. For many of us being broken is not as impending as Marsha's bout with a bruised self-esteem. Sometimes the episode of breaking can be totally unexpected—one moment on top of the world, the other desiring to be under it. This was the experience of Jacob. He was adept at always getting ahead, cheating the system and taking advantage of others. This lifestyle soon led to his arrival in a place of utter disbelief at unrelenting misfortune despite his attempts to do the right thing.

The story of Jacob began somewhat as a topsy-turvy situation. He was born second, and even in birth grasped on to his twin brother's heel. Jacob, whose name literally meant supplanter, even at birth, seemingly sought a way by which he could displace his brother. He sought a way by which he could come in first. There is something about human nature that inclines toward selfish satisfaction. Sin has conditioned us to be thoughtful only for ourselves, from the most insignificant issues to the most important ones we tend to always opt for the path of least resistance to our own comfortability, and toward the outcome that guarantees our victory, or our eventual reward.

As a child Jacob found himself literally on the outskirts of his father's love. The Bible says that Isaac his father loved Esau, but Rebekah loved Jacob. Isn't it something to be the child who just doesn't add up in your father's eyes? Esau was a cunning hunter, a man of the field. He was a man that was naturally skilled in the accouterments of masculine pursuit. However, Jacob was a plain man. As we look at Jacob's background in retrospect we can note a number of factors that serve as a collective premonition of Jacob's eventual season of despair. He was second at birth and he was second in the context of his father's love. He was predisposed or had the proclivity for that which was of little import in his father's eyes. Jacob preferred the comforts of home, living indoors, and working around the kitchen. Jacob looked at his life, and saw Isaac's devotion of fatherly love extended to his brother and not to him. He determined that the only way he could "come up" was to depend on deception. Jacob was coming undone and did not even know it.

Are you a Jacob child? Are you the man or the woman born into this world with an inward desire to lead? Are you the young man who sees yourself as a winner but every goal you go after abruptly ends in failure? Is there a voice deep down inside of you that speaks of great things in you that have not yet been manifested out of you? Maybe you feel that the only way you could get over the slump is if you push someone else out of the way. You might just be coming undone.

The account of Jacob's life gets even murkier when we realize that his mother was a major influence in him developing his character of deception. We can be led many times to make a value and moral judgment against Rebekah because of this new detail about his life. How could this woman, who was blessed to even have a child after being barren for most of her life, then choose to encourage her child to do what appears to put him a moral and spiritual dilemma? Rebekah wasn't just trying to move her son to the head of the pack but rather she thought she was fulfilling the will of God. God is a god of evidential power. He operates in ways that clearly display his glory and his ability to accomplish what he may. God has a purpose behind all that he says or does. The Bible says that Rebekah inquired of the Lord as to why the children in her womb were struggling.

And the Lord said unto her, Two nations are in thy womb, and two manner of people shall be separated from thy bowels; and the one people shall be stronger than the other people: and the elder shall serve the younger.

Genesis 25:23

19

God gave Rebekah a preview of what was to come; He gave her a heads up through a prophetic declaration. I strongly believe that the latter clause of that divine proclamation...and the elder shall serve the younger, was what bore so heavily on Rebekah's mind when she encouraged Jacob to deceitfully pursue his father's blessing. Rebekah was of the mindset that the only way God could perform what He had said about her youngest son was if she gave Him some assistance. God requires no helping hands in the actualizing of his divine destiny for us.

As God assembles the acts of our respective lives we must understand that a word spoken by God about us to others is often times just a mechanism by which God makes others aware of the miracle that he intends to work out in our life. In addition, sometimes a word spoken to you about someone in your life is simply a word that would stand as a witness or a testimony to God's ability to make possible what many thought was impossible in that person's life. Anytime God communicates to you a report of someone's impending greatness, especially a person who at all appearances is unlikely to achieve the stature of that report, it is a word designed not for you to broadcast or orchestrate the outcome. But rather it is a testimony, to alert you to stand still and see the salvation, glory and the power of God accomplish what it will.

Have you ever been thrown into a relationship at the urging of a parent or a friend? Have you done some thing that you have grown to regret because you were simply operating at the behest of someone who said that they were looking out for your best interest? Our lives can become undone when we attempt to walk according to the wishes of others. The person's intentions may be decidedly positive. They may even truly see where God is taking you. But if their mechanism is corrupt it also corrupts the outcome. Even in kingdom work the end does not justify the means. Good ends never come from evil means. The ends may appear good from one perspective but from any other angle lives may be affected and damaged beyond repair. Greatness achieved by deceitful means is soon diminished.

The source of human error is rooted in the human mind's pursuit of self-realization. The propensity of the human mind is to pursue self-knowledge. We have a predilection to being self-made. This passion for creating ones image and for having total control over the reputation that is displayed to the world is birthed in God's original intent and composition for man. The Bible teaches us that in the very beginning God created mankind in His image, and His likeness. Image speaks of our appearance, and likeness speaks of our endowed abilities. We were created so as to be the manifest image of God in the earth, and to be able to work in the earth as He did in the capacity of a creative force. Our inner desire to be self-made stems from the way we were created. God is the uncaused first cause. Man was made in His image and His likeness that means that we were made not to be gods but we were made to be like gods. There is a difference between being a thing and being like a thing. We were made to bring order to disorder, and to manage what God has set in motion not direct the motion but rather supervise it so that there are no distractions from the divine destiny.

Jacob and his mother, Rebekah, wanted to make what God prophesied come to pass by their own power. The things that he experienced that led to his eventual separation from family and escape from the wrath of his brother was due to mismanagement of a Word from God spoken to his mother. God works through us, but not according to us. We are vessels by which he establishes his good will but if we get out of his will; He will readily use another available vessel. Many of us think that we have to do the great work of getting ourselves into the place of prosperity. But we should never lose sight and understanding of the fact that our experience of blessedness and prosperity that comes with salvation cannot be earned by our works, but comes only by faith.

For by grace are ye saved through faith; and that not of yourselves: it is the gift of God. Not of works, lest any man should boast.
Ephesians 2:8,9

Rebekah got a word from the Lord when she sought his face in her time of need. God gave her an answer. He bestowed on her a gift. Jacob was a gift to which was attached favor. It was a favor that was necessary to establish a chosen generation and mark the birth of a great nation. Jacob was destined for greatness just as his mother was eagerly anticipating and engineering. However, her machinations and meddling created greater harm than good. Her actions caused a breach in the family that would eventually lead to Jacob suffering through some things that he really didn't have to deal with. But even in the struggle God worked it out for Jacob's eventual good. Even in your struggle, even after a bad decision that may alter the present and immediate future circumstances of your life you have to know that what God said still stands. If God said that you will be great or He says that your eventual posture will be that of the head and not the tail; He is able to bring that destined position to pass. We must count every setback as a setup for a mighty comeback.

Notes on "Dealing with Becoming Undone"
1. What are the signs?

Coming undone is a natural occurrence in any maturing and developing creature. In order for us to grow physically our bodies have to go through a level of undoing. Our bones become undone at the joints as new cartilage grows in, and old cartilage is transformed into permanent bone. Our muscles literally have to be exhausted and brought to the end of their capacity to do work before they can expand and grow. So it is in the spirit. Our spirits must become undone so that the Spirit of God could enter in.

The signs of your life coming undone can range from the "Why is nothing happening for me?" attitude to the "Will I ever come out of this sentiment?" The lack of evidence of success could be in your relationships, your finances, your career, your social life and, if

22

you're in school, your academic life. This however, is not an indication that your fate is failure, but rather is a sign that God's ready to rearrange some things in your life. Always keep it in mind that falling isn't failure, it's staying down once you've fallen that is an indication of failure. As long as you are able to get up, dust yourself off and realize that there is still a destination in which you are heading and it isn't where you are right now you are far from a failure.

2. *What should you do?*
Worship

Render to God what is due to Him. Worship is the most difficult thing for men and women to understand and to truly enter into today because it is the thread that most tied us to our maker before the fall.

Worship is spiritual. God said that they that worship Him must worship him in Spirit and in truth. Adam worshipped God in Spirit and in truth. But when sin entered the equation the thread of worship was severed. Between God and Adam worship was a singularly spiritual act of God's divine Spirit addressing Adam's human spirit.

Worship was all Adam did because all he did was what God willed Him to do. Worship is to live, move and have your being in God's will. To worship is to give all that you have which is worthwhile to God. It is to give without withholding anything and without expecting anything in return, but trusting that God will sustain you in your surrendering all.

Worship was natural for Adam because that was his lifestyle. Adam lived as a spirit being housed in a physical body that experienced the natural world through the interaction of his soul and his flesh and experienced God through his spirit. His spirit had precedence over his flesh. Hence he walked around physically naked and had no need for coats to keep warm or cottons to keep cool because he was not as aware of his physical needs as he was of his spiritual need. His spiritual senses were more powerful than his physical senses. Why was man more spiritual than he was physical? It was because he became a living soul only after the spiritual breath of God was breathed into him. (Gen. 2:7) Therefore his first experience of life was under the unction of the Holy Spirit. Also as long as his spiritual duties were performed God handled the physical.

23

Worship was easy for Adam because his spirit led the way, and his soul and flesh were under its control. But the first act of sin was a deliberate attempt to disrupt the order of God's intent for man to operate. After the deception, and Adam's eventual act of disobedience the order was rearranged. Flesh took the lead, the soul followed and the spirit brought up the rear. Immediately they were aware that their flesh was exposed although it had always been. Then fear took up residence in their souls because they now chose to hide from the presence of God. The fact that God had to ask them where they were, showed that his spiritual connection to them had been severed. They were spiritually dead to him and therefore unable to properly worship.

I said all of that to say this, that worship is no more physical than eating ice cream is spiritual. Worship for us has to become a practice of bringing our fleshly and soulish desires under subjection and giving God all. Worship is not limited to a certain type of song, or dance, or particular way that you raise your hand or sway or even speak well of Him. Worship is more about how you render your heart to God. David was a man after God's own heart. He wasn't that highly esteemed because of how he dressed or because of how he always said the right things but because he simply went after God's heart in all that he did. He always sought for the hand of God and for the voice of God even in the midst of a messed up situation. Worship is impossible if we withhold from God in the midst of it. Our bodies, our souls and our spirits must all be handed over to Him so that He could put them back into right working order. Worship is rendered best from a prepared vessel. A prepared vessel is one that has been broken through praise, because praise prepares you for entering beyond the veil for more than just admiration. It gives you the power beyond the veil to reverence God and not to be just overwhelmed by His radiance. True worship gets you in His presence while still standing here on earth, just as Adam did in the garden. **(For more on *worship* study the following biblical   text: John 4:20-24; 1 Chron.16:29; Hebrews 1:6; John 9:30-38; Matt. 15:25; Matt. 28:17; Rev. 4:10,11)**

Wait

But they that wait upon the Lord shall renew their strength; they shall mount up with wings as eagles; they shall run, and not be weary; and they shall walk, and not faint.

Isaiah 40:31

Waiting is probably the most difficult *action* that we could take in this life. This is because we fail to see the evidence of action in our wait. We see waiting as inactivity rather than active positioning for the overflow. Remember, the human attribute of wanting to be self-made lights a fire in us that drives us to actively pursue more advantageous outcomes. If we find ourselves in a difficult situation we always look for ways that we could grab onto something floating by, or something within arms length above our heads to hold onto and pull ourselves to safety. To wait for many of us is to frustrate our self-will. But to wait can be the best thing that we do for ourselves in many of the situations that we find ourselves in because it allows God space to set forth His will. It is not that God needs us to make room for Him because He can forcefully make room for himself and He does. But He would rather that we voluntarily trust Him to make it happen.

When we wait on God in the midst of becoming undone we are really carefully positioning ourselves to be in the wind of change that comes from God. It takes us paying attention to wild seeds in nature, and even certain kinds of insects. A great percentage of the activity of their lives is spent waiting. They wait for the change in the seasons, or for the change in the direction of the wind. Some seeds even depend on animals to come by so that they could get attached to their fur and therefore be transported from place to place. The eventual place of rest and residence of a seed is totally governed by the affects of things surrounding it. It ends up where the wind wills or where the animal carries it, but wherever it ends up becomes its place of destiny to grow into whatever tree it needs to grow into. It isn't the wind that dictates to the seed or the animal that dictates to the seed its destiny but rather it is part of the eternal plan of God that determines the seeds ultimate destination. A tree only grows where God wills it to grow. The insect in turn that is driven by the force of the wind ends up in places that it has no control over but God wills that there would be provision enough for that insects survival wherever the wind blows it.

As you wait on God, get into position. One who is becoming undone is at their most vulnerable for disaster. It is because ones mode of defense is down and one is depending on the compassion of God to keep you especially when your immune system is out of whack. This is where faith comes in. I've got to trust God even when I don't see the way out. Just because the bridge is covered over with thick visually impenetrable fog doesn't mean that it isn't still in existence, and you can get safely across. However, the invisibility of the bridge creates in us insecurity about the crossing. Faith is a channel of living trust present between God and man. It is a guidance system that assures is that what we know about the path through this trial is more solid than what I feel, see or hear right now. The atmosphere is tainted with the devil's distractions so I must go by what I was taught and not according to my common sense in the midst of the trouble.

The fact that in the book of the prophet Isaiah God declares that they that wait on him shall renew their strength indicates that He is aware that when we start to become undone there will be an experience of weakening. You will feel weak at various times in your life. You'll feel weak physically and you'll feel weak spiritually but renewal of your strength comes only in the wait and not in the work.

The text of scripture also gives us further insight into what it means to wait on the Lord. It says that they that wait upon the Lord shall mount up with wings as eagles. This suggests that in your waiting upon the Lord you shall be equipped with ability to fly over some things. Eagles wings are most effective if they are outstretched upon a good strong wind. As you wait get positioned in the path of God's wind of change. They that wait upon the Lord shall run and not be weary. Again waiting upon the Lord is given characteristics quite different from our idea of inactive waiting. One who waits on the Lord is waiting while running the good race. Waiting suggests a patient, conservative stride. A run that is more concerned with completing the race rather than running speedily. They shall walk and not faint. As you wait on the Lord, you may have to do some walking until God blesses you with a vehicle. But even then you will walk and not be tired.

(For more on *waiting on the Lord* study the following biblical text: 1 Cor. 1:7; Psalm 62:1,5; Lam. 3:25, 26; Psalm 40:1; Psalm 27:14; Psalm 25:5; Hosea 12:6; Psalm 130:5,6; Psalm 69:3; Isaiah 25:9; Isaiah 42:4; Acts 1:4; Isaiah 40:31; Psalm 69:6; Psalm 37:9, 34; Isaiah 64:4; Luke 12:36, 37)

Work

What kind of work can you do? Or what kind of work should you do if you are becoming undone? Work here should not be taken as some form of aid that you are giving God in making you whole but rather this is a work that is necessary in accelerating your entrance into brokenness. Many times we work hard at making our lives add up to what we believe God wants for us. We work hard at keeping the law, we work hard at being morally upright, we work hard at putting up appearances to render ourselves holy in the eyes of men but this is all work that is futile. All of this work is directed at bettering the individual rather than extending outside of that individual and being directed at bettering others. Our work should the work of service to others because we are saved to serve others who are unsaved as we once were.

Broken, *just to be made new*

The only work that we should be doing is what God says we should be doing even if it seems to be tearing us apart. It seems to be tearing us apart because it is work that is designed to make us different. In order for us to be made different we have to change and change is painful work especially for that which is being changed. The work that God gives us and the work that God starts in us despite the possibility that it may cause our undoing to a certain degree is still a work that comes with a guaranteed reward. The reward that God promises far exceeds any temporary joy we may get in some worldly escape from the work. After the worship and the wait we must work the works of the Lord because in doing that we are setting
up someone else to experience the eventual rebirth that we too will experience in the end.

(For more on *doing Christian work* study the following biblical text: Phil. 2:13; 1 Cor. 12:11; 1 Thess. 2:13; Gal. 5:6; Matt. 5:16; Acts 13:2; 2 Cor. 4:17; Heb. 13:21; Jer. 31:16; Phil. 1:6; Heb. 6:10)

3.
The Blessing in Brokenness

The Lord is close to those who are of a broken heart and saves such as are crushed with sorrow for sin and are humbly and thoroughly penitent.

Psalm 34:18 Amplified

Imagine awaking one morning and realizing that all that you have lived for was a lie. I was recently viewing clips from a popular television talk show. And in one of the segments there sat a fairly attractive young lady, a blonde bombshell by all accounts, very sophisticated in her appearance and speaking confidently about a life changing experience that she had. She began to recount to the host what sounded to me like a dream life. She came from a pretty well off background with both of her parents having been highly educated and professionals in their respective fields and as a result her years occupying the nest were days of relative comfort and ease. She wasn't necessarily wealthy but she also wasn't anywhere close to being in the throes of poverty.

A few years after graduating from college she met the most charming man, fell head over heels in love with him and before she knew it they were running down the aisle and she was soon lifted over the threshold into wedded bliss. But the story doesn't end there in fact it really hadn't even begun yet.

She then related a life that sounded like an indefinite honeymoon. He was both a prominent and wealthy physician and had no problem or misgivings about spending inordinate amounts of money on her--lavishing her with gifts and insisting that she need not seek employment. How much better can it get? The farthest thing from her mind was betrayal. The farthest thing from her mind was the thought that this man really was not who he said or who he appeared to be.

And the day that her life took a change for the worst was probably the most unlikely timing on her part. It was her thirtieth birthday if I recall correctly and her husband had planned an over the top celebration. He was going to fly her and a group of her closest friends and family to the Greek Islands and on his private yacht somewhere out among the European isles he was going to give her the best birthday she ever had. But on the days leading up to the big trip she commented that he started to act strange. He was very moody and would walk around seemingly depressed. What could it be? He had the wealth. He had the gorgeous wife. He had the prominence. He had the prestige as a leader in his field. But yet still he was troubled in his conscience. Nevertheless, the day of the trip came and all involved were jetted off to the European isles and everything seemed to be on track. But everything for this woman was actually about to be derailed. She was about to be knocked totally off the track and on to the dangerous third rail of rejection.

On that first morning after arriving on the Greek coast her beloved, wealthy and supposedly best friend of a husband was no where to be found. They had gone to bed together that night but in the morning she rose and he was gone from next to her never to be seen again. Can you imagine the sensation that must have gone through this woman? How it must have been a few days later or a week or even a month after when she realized that this man who had been the bearer of her dreams, and the answer to her childhood aspirations to be treated like a queen was gone?

Everything she had taken for granted as the wife of the wealthy doctor now hung in the balance. Every convenience that she had grown to expect over the years was now potentially unavailable to her. She changed from a picture of confidence to a visage of brokenness-with tear soaked eyes and tear-stained cheeks. From where she stood and given what she was saying at this point in her life she could never see the blessing in her breakup. She could never see that this episode was for her eventual good because all that she was feeling now was an emptiness that brought with it sadness. This woman was broken. She was wounded in the seat of her emotions. She was left with the proverbial "why" and the desire for that why to be answered as if the answer would relieve the pain. As if it would somehow restore what she now saw as great loss.

This woman's story is the story of many of us today, rich or poor, prominent or obscure—the most difficult task for us is to recover from the train wreck of brokenness. And before recovery could begin we also have to get to the place where we even see the likelihood of restoration taking place, and of this all being a lesson to make us better men, women, or children.

Can you stand to be broken, just to be made new? Can God possibly have a blessing of renewal in store for me even in the moment or occasion of my utter wounding? When one considers the likelihood of experiencing the episode of brokenness we must really ask ourselves questions concerning the kind of perspective that we should keep in these incidences. Believers and unbelievers alike must agree that a life lived is a life that has seen its share of broken promises, dashed expectations and wounded spirits.

There is no prerequisite of salvation or spiritual rebirth in order for one to be entangled in brokenness. But there is a spiritual requirement for one to come out on the other side of it all, better off than when you entered in. If you entered in spiritually sick and God allowed the encumbrance of brokenness then He intended it to be an eye opening experience that would bring you to an understanding of your fragility in his presence. He did it so that you would come to a place where you saw your dependence on Him as paramount to you experiencing life in its fullness. However, if your experience of brokenness were a direct result of your willful practice of sin, your appreciation for the blessing hidden in brokenness would be far less likely. In this case you could only see the negative side to the brokenness. You could only see what you are losing rather than what you are gaining. You can only see what you are being deprived of and not what you are actually being preserved from.

What does it mean to be broken in the eyes of God? We live in a day and age when to accept brokenness is considered a sign of failure, it is seen as short changing oneself. We throw away most items the moment they become broken. Gone are the days when an incident of an item becoming broken meant that a repairman of some sort would be employed to fix the problem. The age of repairmen included repairs of items as small as jewelry, and watches, to shoes, and appliances, and especially to automobiles. However, today the repairman is a rare commodity. This is due to the advent of self-help books, do-it-yourself guides and the plain just-buy-a-new-one philosophy. We find it hard to stand and wait for repairs to be done to something that has been broken. The work of a repairman is no longer valued. We would rather spend the money to purchase it entirely new.

We throw away the broken goods of our life and we look to buy new goods. The Bible says in Revelation 21 that He that sits upon the throne says, "Behold I make all things new!" It also says that we should walk in the newness of life and serve in the newness of spirit. We have to understand that the bible does speak of experiencing the new, and of living in the new. It speaks of the new commandment to love one another, of the new covenant, of us being a new creation, of the new fruit, of a new name and of God doing a new thing

But we must also understand that there is something that comes before the new. There are some things in us that must be broken, and then mended into that new thing. God is concerned about the residue that remains after our hour of brokenness because it is upon this residue that He builds our new life. Before I experience the new, I must break free of the old. God is concerned about your heart. He is diligently seeking the hearts of men to see who is in pursuit of His heart. God judges the contents of your heart and not your outward man. He judges the contents of your heart and not of your bank account. He judges your heart and not even your mind, because your mind can usually be the thing that takes you on a path away from God.

Now that we've come to an understanding of the necessity of us experiencing brokenness, how do we find the blessing in it? How do we overcome the thoughts of regret and the painful feelings that come with it and grow to appreciate the blessing that God has placed in the midst of the brokenness? How do I begin to channel the hurt of a wounded spirit to see that there is a measure of good in it that far outweighs the bad that I feel?

We could never do justice to the subject of brokenness without ever referring to the biblical teaching and the perfect example given unto us with regard to the subject as per the life of Jesus Christ. You may be reading this book and find yourself in the camp of those who would consider themselves unbelievers. However, that does not negate the fact that the story of his life is one that speaks of complete goodwill. The facts as they stand related by Christians worldwide or as according to essential Christian doctrine backed by quantifiable leagues of historical evidence profess of a life that was phenomenally good in relation to any human standard of moral correctness. Recognizing the example of his professed life is fundamental to ones understanding of the idea of living in the blessings of brokenness. Just to think of the sacrifice that Jesus had to endure as God.

He had to contend with collapsing the immensity that he was to the insufficiency that man was. We get a peek into the blessedness of brokenness every time we consider the trial of scorn he went through from his own people on the account of his assignment here among us. Jesus was the blessed of the Lord; in fact we believe that He was the expressed substance of God's announced blessing upon the earth. He declared that He was called to minister salvation, healing and deliverance to the brokenhearted. He was the great physician sent to bring healing to all that were broken. Believe in God or not, believe in Jesus' deity or not and you still have to recognize that He did many great indisputable wonders and signs to restore wholeness to many a broken man and woman.

Jesus said if you don't believe in me; believe on me just for my works sake. This is not a discourse to convince you to believe in Jesus Christ but rather to bring you to a place where you can appreciate the places where praise is necessary on your part even when you feel the pain of being broken. You don't have to be a Christian to appreciate that there must an inkling of joy somewhere in that rebellious child rejecting your authority and making a run for it on there own. It can't all be gloom and doom because that would mean that life is essentially unfair. You don't have to be a believer, to feel deep down in your soul that it probably was a good thing that the relationship didn't work out. That relationship in which you had so much invested and that didn't work out because deep on the inside, you found out that you were doing things that were compromising your integrity.

Relishing the blessing at a time when it is easier for one to weep takes a latent strength that goes far beyond physical prowess. It is a spiritual thing. It takes spiritual muscles to see God's good will in the midst of your soulish desires being quenched. The wife who finds out that her husband has cheated, the scars that are dealt by infidelity by either party in a marriage can often so hurt the individuals ego and their sense of worth that they miss the blessing in the betrayal. To even speak about it seems like an oxymoron, blessing in a betrayal. But we have to believe that it must be providence that made this discovery possible especially for those women or men who just have no idea that their mate has been less than honest to them. We have to see the providence in severe sickness that causes one to give account of their priorities in life.

The blessing in brokenness is to be found in the salvation it brings. Sometimes being broken could be an avenue by which God alerts us to, and saves us from the ultimate demise that we were destined to fall into sometime down the line if we had stayed in the place we were in. Being broken can be a method by which God fixes someone's eyes on him.

What does Jesus say about being broken? What does he teach about the concept of preparatory trial sanctioned by God? When we get into a discussion or a discourse on brokenness as it pertains to the calling of God upon our lives we must make clear distinctions from the harmful acts that are designed by the enemy to destroy us, and the providential will of God designed to equip us. The Bible teaches us as according to the foundational text for this chapter that God is attracted to them that are of a broken heart and he saves such as are of a contrite spirit. It is brokenness that God desires to search the motives of our heart. Are we in this thing just for the luxuries that it may afford us? Are we in it for the prestige or the reverential treatment that we may receive when others recognize the calling on our lives? Or are we questionable when others can't see what God said about us? It is in the season of brokenness that God is made privy to the genuine content of our heart. It is in this time that all that we are is unashamedly laid bare in the presence of God's awesome glory. Jesus said that he came to bind up the brokenhearted and to proclaim liberty to the captives. As we approach to gain an understanding of the Master's take on brokenness I am led to examine one of his many parables that I believe speaks volumes on God's intention in imputing upon his true sons and daughters the experience of brokenness.

Hear another parable: There was a certain householder, which planted a vineyard, and hedged it round about, and digged a winepress in it, and built a tower, and let it out to husbandmen, and went into a far country:

Matthew 21:33

In most biblical text this is referred to as the parable of the householder demanding fruit from his vineyard. In our study of scripture symbolism we can make a clear parallel and assume that the vineyard represents a sanctified people, a chosen people. We may be even tempted to say that the vineyard represents the church. The householder hedged his vineyard around. He literally planted a hedge around the circumference of his vineyard to protect it from the intrusion of enemies. In addition to the protection around the vineyard the householder, God, dug a winepress in the center of the vineyard. Then last and certainly not least he built a tower in the midst.

This imagery is chock full of meaning. The householder, God, has made a wall of protection around his people. He has dug a place in the center of our lives where he might work some things out of us. He has also built a high place from which we can sit and watch for the coming enemies and for the returning master. All these things he has left in the hands of a few chosen men and women of God, whom he has called to manage his creation. What does this all have to do with brokenness? How does this illustrate or communicate the significance of brokenness in the ultimate plan of God?   The Bible teaches us that whenever Jesus spoke a parable he was taking an earthly concept to explain a heavenly principle. The householder is God and if we were to pay close attention to the actions that this householder takes in setting his affairs straight before departing we can clearly see the hidden truth of the purposed will of God. As the householder plants so too does God plant. As the householder, protects, God protects. And as the householder establishes a place of preparation for the harvest, God establishes a place of preparation. And it is in the establishing of this place of preparation that we see the hand of God in brokenness.

It is in the winepress that the grapes that are chosen for harvesting are tossed and treaded upon to get the juice out of them. How many of you out there reading this book, and consider yourselves children of God know that there is a place in the center of your life that was established simply as your place of pressing. The place where you are pushed until the best that God has deposited inside of you is forced to come out. Inevitably in the press impurities will be forced to come out as well. When you study the production of wine it is interesting to note that even in the press the greatest care is taken not to damage the seed because crushed seeds in a batch of grapes would cause the wine to sour and sour wine is only good for vinegar.

Broken, *just to be made new*

The winepress is a significant part of the vineyard, just as the trial and trouble that we face in this life that leads to brokenness in us, is a significant part of what God planned for us. God desires to forge new wine out of us but before he could do that we must be broken. There are some things in us that must be broken because as long as they stand unbroken they are rendered ineffective. Like an undissolved antacid pill lying in an upset stomach, the things that serve, as our avenues to healing that lay unbroken in our spirits will cause no change in our ailment. In order for these pills to work they must be broken, and their contents allowed freely flow through our bodies. In order for us to experience true healing there are some pills deposited in our spirits that need decomposition and breaking.

We stand in the vineyard, we see the grapes and we taste the wine but we lose sight of the process that exists in the in-between. Before we experience the new we must break free of the old. A breaking must occur. We see ourselves in the new, we anticipate victory and rightly so but we totally overlook the breaking that has to take place in between receiving the word of the promise and experiencing the reality of the promise. The often disputed, writer of the book of Hebrews in scripture says that after we patiently endure, we will obtain the promise. The breaking is a test. It is a test that produces patience; a patience that ends in a perfect and complete work. Dough has to be beaten and broken and broken and beaten and then put to sit in the heat of the oven before you get perfectly baked bread.

An athlete has to have his threshold of pain, and performance and stamina broken before he could partake of the greater. His breathing increases, his heart rate rises, his pulse races and his chest hurts. His muscles ache as lactic acid is built up in them and he begins to tire. His legs feel like they can't go anymore. His arms feel like they can't lift another weight. He's "maxed" out. He's broken. But all he has to do is take a rest. Just one day off, and return to the gym just two days later and watch how much weight he pushes this time. His body has broken the threshold, and has now set a new goal for that physique to reach. He loads up the barbell with ten more pounds on either side and he lifts. It isn't easy but he does more than he did two days ago. Why? His arms have broken the threshold of pain and he is lifting with new strength.

Can you stand to be broken just to be made new? The Old Testament gives us an account of the life of one of scriptures' most charismatic figures, King David. If there was any character in the entire history of the Bible who had a guaranteed promise of a great end it was David. The Prophet of the Lord anointed David at the age of eighteen to be king, but he did not step into that position until he had gone through twelve years of trial, testing and breaking. He was called from the sheepfold, anointed to be king and sent back to take care of the sheep. He achieved a sudden peak of infamy for his handling of Goliath but after that he was relegated to the status of the palace musician. He was hunted and persecuted by the very man whom he had grown to admire as a role model, the now spiritually deposed King Saul. But it was all in an effort to break any inkling of pride and mentality of being self-made that may have been lodged in his spirit.

When we look at the story of David we see how brokenness can be a time of loneliness. Every form of support but God was removed. His family was gone. His father and brothers had other problems of their own that they had to deal with. Samuel the Prophet of God was gone. Ahimelech the High Priest of God was gone. Saul his mentor was definitely gone and in fact had become hostile to him. Jonathan his best friend still torn between loyalty to his father and loyalty to his friend could not be depended upon. David had to be broken of his dependency on others in order for him to be made new as he drew closer to God. This is lived out in the testimony of the psalms that he penned during this season in his life.

What is your testimony? What is your witness? Is it a witness that speaks only of the material things that God has given you? Or is it a testimony that speaks of brokenness for God's sake? Is your witness one of boasting of your spiritual achievements or your good works? Is it a witness of you being saved and sanctified? Or is it a witness of brokenness mentally, morally and spiritually for the sake of Jesus Christ? Can you stand to be spoilt in this life; spoilt in the eyes of men only to be made new in the eyes of God? The apostle Paul said in his second epistle to the Corinthian church, "Though the more abundantly I love you, the less I be loved." When we love in the natural we expect some love in the return. But Paul says although I know that I get no love in return I still love you more. That is the God type of love. This is the love that is birthed in brokenness; the love that appreciates the faithfulness of a just and holy God. This is the love that drives our spirit to say though he slay me I will trust Him. Can you stand to be broken in the name of love? Paul did.

Notes on "The Blessing in Brokenness"
1. *How am I supposed to see the good in a really dark place?*

The dire circumstances that we face in life can greatly color our appreciation of the gift that life is. Each new day that we are allowed to see, or in which we are allowed to partake of life's pleasures or to walk in life's freedoms is a day that God gives us an opportunity to see Him in his creation. However, when discomfort becomes a part of that walk we can many times lose sight of the divine education that is taking place. Even in our tight places there is something to be learned that ultimately will bring us to a greater intimacy with a gracious God. Be it in hospital, or in a literal prison or be it in the prison of our minds; even in our times of brokenness God can teach us something. And the lesson that he teaches under those circumstances is a blessing because you could have been cut off and there is no learning beyond the grave. These lessons are not merely academic courses that must be stored away in some filing cabinet assigned to our spiritual transcript but should be a lesson that we

39

utilize to transform our lives, and then tell others about so that they may transform their own lives. Deal with your experience of brokenness, look for the blessing that God is communicating through it and learn from it. Then take that lesson and teach someone else about it.

4.

Pained for a Purpose

The Lord is merciful and gracious, slow to anger, and plenteous in mercy. He will not always chide: neither will he keep his anger for ever. He hath not dealt with us after our sins; nor rewarded us according to our iniquities.
For as the heaven is high above the earth, so great is his mercy toward them that fear him.

Psalm 103:8-11

Why do good people die young? Why do they suffer such tragic deaths? Why did God let her die? Why did he have to die that way? Why did they have to suffer the way that they did? Why did so many innocent people have to die? Why am I going through such tension? Why the troubles at work, the bills, the tumor? Why? The questions alone could be compiled into a book. The questions that we could ask God concerning our lives and our experiences under his will, if we were ever given the opportunity to do so could stretch for miles from end to end. These questions swim around in the mind of both the believer and the unbeliever, even if their understanding of God is limited by their inability to see him by faith.

41

The incidences that cause these questions to arise in our minds may include the sudden death of one dare to us, the passing of a young child, a troubling medical diagnosis or a soured marriage relationship. The questions become even more laced with passion when these things happen to one who professes to be a child of God. It seems today as if cancer is rampant in the body of Christ with more people having prayer requests for healing from this deadly disease than any other naturally occurring ailment. As a Christian, a believer in Jesus Christ we tend to come to the conclusion that we are being punished for some past or secret sin. As we continue to dissect the idea of God ordained brokenness I believe that we should take some time to deal with the possibility of being pained for a purpose.

I strongly believe that God does all that he does and allows all that he allows on purpose, for purpose and by purpose. As long as we live in this dispensation or this divine era of grace I find it hard to believe that God is rendering punishment upon us or judging us when we face trouble. This is especially hard to believe when we are walking according to what we know to be the will of God. We can't blame suffering in the world on the anger of God. He's not mad. He didn't mess up. He does not make mistakes. And we don't even have the moral capacity to disappoint God. God expects us to fail if we operate on our own, and doesn't like to see us fail but he knows it is part of us being subject to corruption. God doesn't aimlessly dole out punishment. In his court there is no miscarriage of justice.

So why do we suffer? If God is merciful and omniscient, and omnipotent and just, why does it *feel* that life is so unfair? It is just simply because God is sovereign. In his sovereignty God has allowed pain into your life to advance his purposes. Your problems, struggles, headaches, heartaches and your hassles are all toward his glory and for his good pleasure.

Broken, *just to be made new*

Work out your own salvation with fear and trembling. For it is God which worketh in you both to will and to do of his good pleasure.
Philippians 2:12-13

From as far back as I can remember my grandmother who raised me was a Bible-believing, church going virtuous woman, loving mother and faithful wife but also for just as long I have known her to be in the midst of struggle, suffering and trial. Be it in the way of a poverty stricken childhood, curtailed adolescents, an unfaithful husband—having to take on the role of caretaker when she herself was still a child and untrustworthy friendships that contributed to the dysfunction in her marriage. My grandmother as far as I had seen it just had pure bad luck. But yet still she stayed faithful to God, reading His word, in constant prayer and immersing herself in the church. I could not see the use in it all. Pregnant with her first child at the age of fifteen, married that same year against the wishes of many. And struggling financially in those first few years but still confident that she had done what was best. She believed that she was in God's will. But God's will seemingly was bringing with it added pain at almost every step. After several years and 10 children later the first two of who died in childbirth, my grandmother was left alone, a single mother. She was now responsible solely for the care of 8 children and a few grandchildren, including myself.

Why did she have to go through what she went through? Why was she subjected to such seeming contradictions to her faith? Our natural conclusion would be to believe that she was being punished for some past or secret sin. But we have to always keep in mind that God does not operate with us from a position of vengefulness, even if we are in a state of sin.

The Lord is merciful and gracious, slow to anger, and plenteous in mercy. He will not always chide: neither will he keep his anger for ever.

Hugh J Harmon

He hath not dealt with us after our sins; nor rewarded us according to our iniquities.

For as the heaven is high above the earth, so great is his mercy toward them that fear him.

Psalm 103:8-11

I believe that Grandma went through what she went through because she was selected to struggle. God, in his very nature as the epitome of love, carries before him mercy and grace, and continually offers them to us. And within that grace and mercy God has devised ways by which he can birth great faith in us even in the midst of turmoil, faith that is immediately visible to the world. And this is the type of faith that he birthed in my Grandma.

We live in a day where it seems by all appearances that the enemy is greatly rewarding those who diligently do his work. Many times we look at the saints of God, the believers and we seldom see the rewards equated to that of the world. Frankly we don't see what we would expect to be part of the benefits of a good life. As a result, many believers have grown weary in well doing. But what if God was allowing hardship in some, to show others how one that believes God should handle life when the comfort of things or people is no longer available and only God can be relied upon. In the face of derision she stood still. When her husband left, she stood still. When some of her children began to go through adolescent rebellion, she stood still. When she was laid off of her job, she stood still. She was picked out, to be picked on because God knew that she was going to stand out on his Word. She stood out by faith. She stood still because that on which she stood was a firm foundation that was built to weather any storm. When the storms come and all that you have is shaken and possibly even broken remember that after the storm the sun rises again. Also remember that what was broken in the storm was only making way for that which is new.

44

Broken, *just to be made new*

The trend towards materialism especially in western culture has made inroads into the western church and as a result, the church is slowly adopting many of the same standards as the world when it comes to evaluating success. The special significance that is given to the experience of brokenness is lost in a world that treasures possessions and positions over the One that possesses. We have begun to live lives emaciated of faith and solely based on sensory-based belief. The motto has started to become "seeing is believing". If we can't see it now we start to believe that it just is never going to happen and we simply have to settle and be contented with what we have. God is slowly being relegated to some stingy, miserly tyrant who doles out wealth only to those who are highly educated and able to manipulate the world system. Faith has become a 'bad word', almost an archaic term for a castle or a pie in the sky. Those who live by true biblical faith are subjected to ridicule; some are even considered bewitched. The meaning of faith now sounds more like fate. We put greater faith in failure than we do in success because we know that failure comes easy. It takes no work to fail that comes simply by inactivity. Forfeiture is a failure. Dreams are no longer being coaxed into existence through powerful applications of faith.

We are resigned to artfully maneuver our way to higher salaries through manipulation and falsehood. We apply for loans on credit, fudge the numbers, pretend separation from spouses and deny streams of income so that we could weasel our way to a promissory note from a lender. We hang our hopes on medical practitioners to cure us and we forsake prayer and the laying on of hands that may heal us. We visit family members in crisis-jail, hospital, or just simply grieving; and prayers are nothing more than an afterthought. God is slowly being pushed out of the screenplay we call life. His role is slowly but surely shrinking. But thank God for his love toward us. That he would think enough of us to stop in the midst of our mess and cause us to turn our faces back to him. It is in our moments or seasons of breaking that God causes some of us to turn our faces back to him. The trial is to break you not to wound you.

When life's outcomes seem to continually render to us contradictions of our faith; the thought of rebellion against God can sometimes tug at our conscience. Some of us grow up in such dire straits that when we do come to faith in Jesus Christ we expect a miraculous turnaround or at least a life that stands directly contrary to what we've been accustomed to. And we expect this to occur with little effort on our part. This is natural and is actually a very good attitude to have toward the walk of salvation. But a good attitude doesn't always equal sound doctrine. We may have a good attitude but if our expectations of God are skewed we will never truly get into the place he would have us to be.

However, oftentimes it isn't so much the external elements of our life that has created our dysfunctional status but rather it is our own view of self. We come to Christ, and we unconsciously lay our expectations of him in very much the same realm as we did with our natural father. We expect that if we fail to live up to his standard, that we will not only disappoint him, but we will also be punished by him as our parents did and our spouses did. I am going to say something that you've probably never heard before. You can't disappoint God. People, friends and family can all be disappointed in you and many times rightly so. But you can't disappoint God. I must repeat it, you can't disappoint God. To disappoint Him would be to suggest that God in some way did not know that we were capable of failure. God doesn't want us to fail but He also knows that without Him we are destined to fail. God wants us to come to a place of complete surrender so that he could work through us, his good pleasure for us. The work that we do is a work done in, by and through the power of Jesus.

Brokenness becomes necessary for us when our view of God and our relationship to Him is based on our knowledge and experience of the natural relationships of our past. God is our spiritual father. He is the supremely wise father of us all. The best father in the world cannot approach God in his exclusive greatness as a father. One good test of whether you still have unbrokenness in you is to quiz yourself about what you feel a father is. If your image of fatherhood is based on adjectives such as harsh taskmaster, rigid, cruel, quick to punish-your view of God, most likely (statistically speaking), is in the same realm. As long as we keep these rather subjective ideas of fatherhood in mind we will continue to unconsciously rate God on this strict scale. Even an early life that is marked by loose unrestrained relationships with fathers, or situations where your father was totally anti-discipline or uninvolved in the rearing of their own children, gives a distorted perspective that can translate to our view of God. It is natural for man to impute to God the qualities of our earthly father especially when we enter into relationship with God from a child to father perspective.

The Bible holds within its pages many examples of men and women whose possible distorted views of their natural fathers led to God orchestrating circumstances in their lives so as to bring brokenness. For some of them it wasn't solely their natural fathers but more so their view of the adult males in their life. In this chapter selected to struggle we will examine the story of a few biblical characters whose lives were marked either by an episode of spiritual brokenness or episodes of spiritual breaking. These characters also exhibit almost a proclivity to brokenness, which I believe serves as an indication of their great significance to the plan of God. These men and women became stalwarts of faith—toward which all men can look for direction when living in a season of distress. When in distress especially when you believe that you are doing the right thing in the answer is not rebellion; or unbelief but rather it is to hold on to the faithful Word of God.

47

Hugh J Harmon

Where can we find this type of faith? The story of
Moses starts out as much in obscurity, as it ended in glory.
Moses, the great deliverer of the Hebrew nation from
bondage in Egypt started out as a child abandoned on the
river Nile in the bulrushes, with hopes that upon discovery
he would be afforded a better life than what laid ahead of
him as the offspring of a slave.

> *And there went a man of the house of Levi, and took to wife a*
> *daughter of Levi.*
> *And the woman conceived, and bare a son: and when she saw him*
> *that he was a goodly child, she hid him three months.*
>
> Exodus 2:1,2

Moses' father was unnamed, simply his familial ties are
mentioned. This is much the same story as many young
men and women of today. The only remnant of the father's
presence in the lives of their children is in the child's
surname or given name.

The first damage to be done to Moses' perception of
fathers, and the act that would set up his necessity for
eventual brokenness was in his father's almost invisibility in
his early life. It was so evident that his mother was left to
determine a scheme to assure his survival. Where was
Moses' father in this whole episode? Didn't he have any
input into what was to become o his son? Did he not care?
Fortunately or unfortunately, I've still yet to decide, this
sentiment is one that I am quite familiar with. I've had the
distinct privilege of being a mentor, teacher and coach to
young men who have had the same questions for much of
my adult life. Ultimately, these young men will have to be
coached through their eventual seasons of brokenness. This
is where the distinction must be made between being broken
and being wounded. A bruised spirit is a spirit that has
taken a blow has some discoloration may even be broken but
is not permanent. While a wounded spirit is a spirit that has
been violently damaged leaving a permanent scar. These
young men possess wounded spirits all stemming from a

disconnect from, and disillusionment with their absent fathers.

Moses is eventually adopted into the Pharoah's household as a son. Therefore, he begins to look for the idea of father in the Pharoah. But deep down on the inside Moses knew that this man was not His father. He also knew that the moment he did not live up to this man's expectation he could potentially lose all that he had grown accustomed to. Moses must have also felt that Pharoah really didn't have to keep him. Many of our boys living in homes with blended families (families made up of step-parents and their kids from previous relationships and kids from a marriage all living together) feel the tension. The feel the tension of living up to the expectations of a stepfather, a man who to them is essentially a stranger with no blood ties.

Tension in many a home of a blended family can be directly blamed on the insecurities of children about their purpose and position in a family headed by a stepfather. Moses in a tense position knew his delicate status as a privileged adopted son, but also recognizing the plight of his people. The duality of emotions that raged in Moses led him to make what seemed to be a virtuous decision. He killed an Egyptian that had wronged a fellow Israelite. And this decision led to the fulfilling of the fears he may have had about disappointing his adopted father.

Now when Pharaoh heard this thing, he sought to slay Moses. But Moses fled from the face of Pharaoh, and dwelt in the land of Midian: and he sat down by a well.

Exodus 2:15

But even in our miscalculations and rash decisions we must know that God is still working it out for our good, especially if we are doing what we truly believe to be the right thing. God does not punish us according to our ignorance, rather he deals with us according to our knowledge. In other words, God would never hold us in judgment for something in which we had no idea we were doing wrong. We also have to trust and believe that when we get down to nothing, God is up to something.

Moses, in a state of obvious guilt for what he had done, was a prime candidate for brokenness. Especially given the fact that he was forced to come to the realization of guilt by the accusation of the very ones whom he had intended to help through his actions. Raised in the lap of luxury, trained by the finest teachers of his age, and separated from the persecution that his people faced could have easily given Moses a greater than necessary view of himself. Pride was knocking at the door; and he needed an infusion of humility. Beware of actions done in self-righteousness because they soon divert us from God's righteousness.

It is interesting what happens next. Moses meets the daughters of the priest of Midian, and after helping them to gather water for their father's flock, they return to their father and tell him about Moses. The interesting part is how the daughters of Midian describe Moses as an Egyptian. Even after the murder, done in the name of saving his fellow man, and escaping to the wilderness. Moses couldn't shake his appearance. He still looked like what he no longer wanted to be identified with. He had to be broken.

And they said, An Egyptian delivered us out of the hand of the shepherds, and also drew water enough for us and watered the flock.
Exodus 2:19

Moses was selected to struggle. The pain that he was to face in life was for a purpose. He had shown God that he had a heart for his people. He had looked on their burdens, even though he was living a life of privilege. Moses was willing to give up all of his worldly advantage just to relieve the burden of one of his own. He had a heart that was consequently ripe for God's working. Moses literally from the heart was yearning for the people of God just as God himself was.

> And God looked upon the children of Israel, and God had respect unto them.
>
> Exodus 2:25

Moses did a bad deed in the name of righteousness but God used the harsh consequences of this action to correct, redeem, heal and restore Moses' character. God had done so much for him on the upside of things that when he had to face a period of correction for wrong it was relatively easy for him to come back to earth as God molded him.

Has your life to date been a Moses experience? Did you have your daunting beginning changed through the goodwill of virtual strangers? Maybe you've had to deal with uncertain acceptance in a non-traditional family. Your father was hardly around or was completely absent and the man who took his place really just tolerated you. Have you ever done something for someone in the name of love and that same someone rebuked you for having done what you did? You fought a man that you saw abusing your mother or sister and they ended up filing charges on you. You did something that you thought may have been noble, but you ended up on the wrong end of indignation for that very thing. You are a prime candidate for God's breaking. And it's not a breaking to defeat you, but rather it is a breaking designed to force the best out of you.

Up to that point in Moses' life when he met the daughters of Jethro he had had it pretty good. But from that time on he was broken. He was left for 40 years to tend to Jethro's flock—a stranger's wealth, and to realize the walk of humility and meekness. When God would eventually approach him to take on the mission of confronting the powers that be. Moses was stripped of any ego, any personal confidence or self-courage he had left Egypt with some forty years earlier. He no longer looked like an Egyptian. He was now a humble Israelite Shepherd familiar with the backside of the desert.

> *And Moses answered and said, But behold they will not believe me...*
>
> Exodus 4:1a

> *And Moses said unto the Lord, O my Lord, I am not eloquent, neither therefore...but I am slow of speech, and of a slow tongue.*
>
> Exodus 4:10

Subjective humility, or a personal humility is always a sign of the residue of brokenness. Moses could find no good reason in himself as to why God should or would want to use him. Do you? Then maybe, just maybe you're still on the other side of brokenness.

Did Moses' life from this point on transform into a bed of ease? We might expect that given the fact that he was moving in the will of God. But we must remember that as long as we live as flesh, and in this natural world despite us walking in the will of God we will face trouble. Jesus said, in this world you shall face tribulation but be of good cheer for I have overcome the world. Everything in this world fights against the life that is in us. We are living souls that have a body and not bodies that have a living soul. And our bodies exist subject to the natural world. So even though Moses had the favor and companionship of God he still would face resistance and rejection from both the Egyptians and his very own people. But again, he was selected to struggle, and he had been divinely predisposed to rejection by the people but God's will in redeeming his people and taking them to the threshold of his promise was still of greater value than any trouble he may have faced, regardless of how long.

Grandma was selected to struggle with eight kids, uncertain employment and with no man in the house because God was determined to show through her life that he was able to sustain and care for his own. He was determined to show how success in school, careers and ministry could still be garnered from a broken and dysfunctional family. The dysfunctional unorthodox family arrangement is not God's original intent, and man's current state of corruption isn't either, but He is enough God to use this dysfunction to birth true survivors and spirit-filled overcomers.

Another character that exhibits the traits of one selected to struggle, although she is little mentioned in biblical study as an example of brokenness, is Naomi. We are introduced to Naomi in the book of Ruth and she is pretty much thrust into her season of brokenness from the outset.

And Elimelech, Naomi's husband died, and she was left and her two sons.

And Mahlon and Chilion, Naomi's sons died also both of them; and the woman was left of her two sons and her husband.

Ruth 1:3,5

A wife's loss of her husband and a mother's loss of her sons are dual experiences that Naomi is faced with at the outset of this biblical account. Imagine the sense of guilt that she must have felt. The only survivor of her small family; she was destined for certain heartbreak. Her faith was absolutely put to the test. Can we still have faith in a God that allows you the experience of this perceived robbery of those closest to us? Can we trust a God that so wants to be close to us that He takes those who stand in the way, out of His way? Some of us are so fond of each other that we forsake rendering God his due benevolence. This love, and desire for intimacy came from God, and reveals His great care for us. God has equipped us, in such a way, with a love that could potentially cause us to love other things more than we love Him.

How did Naomi overcome this loss? How did she reconcile the hurt feelings she may have felt toward God?

...the hand of the Lord is gone out against me.

Ruth 1:13b

She had concluded that it was because of some iniquity or transgression she had committed against the Lord, this was why she had been recompensed in that way. Many times we mistake the breaking that God affects in our lives as punishment. We are given very little background into Naomi's past. We know nothing about the relationship she had with her husband prior to his death. All we know is that they had left their homeland to escape famine and sojourn in a new land. Therefore, we have to make some suppositions about why God allowed her to experience this loss. It must have been brokenness initiated by God to direct fulfillment of His divine plan. Everything that Naomi went through was orchestrated specifically to make manifest the divine destiny that was tied up in her lineage.

Naomi's relationship with her daughter-in-law, as strange as it may seem to our contemporary standards was integral in her fulfilling her destiny and vice versa. Ruth needed to stay connected to Naomi so that her destiny would be fulfilled, even after her first husband died. The book of Ruth as short as it is contains great symbolism of truth and gives insight to the character of God and his eventual plan for His people. Ruth was a Moabite, a Gentile and outsider. She cleaved to Naomi an Israelite. Ruth heeded Naomi's counsel and was fortunate to marry a kinsman of Naomi. This act of Ruth, and her eventual reward was a redemptive experience for Naomi. This Gentile woman and adopted daughter of Naomi birthed a son from whose line the redeemer of both Israel and the Gentile world would eventually arise.

Naomi's season of brokenness and her patience to deal with a daughter-in-law's persistence to stay under her wing started a chain reaction. God used this situation to bring life back to Naomi and to give Ruth a fresh start.

Broken, *just to be made new*

It's bigger than you and I. The things that we suffer through are more than just incidents designed to cripple us. God has a plan that is much larger than what we can even fathom. Some of us are pained for a purpose and selected to struggle. Your assignment in God's will may just be to suffer pain in the face of others for His glory. What glory is to be won in the face of your suffering, in the face of your struggle, and in the face of disability? Jesus in referring to and correcting an inquiry of the disciples about the source of a blind man's affliction said this man's blindness was an act that provided an opportunity for God's work to be made manifest. God's work of healing and power over blindness needed to be shown, and this man was to be the vehicle by which God was to gain glory. Jesus wants to use you, so that He could get the glory.

5.

Strong in the Broken Places

Finally, my brethren, be strong in the Lord, and in the power of his might.

Ephesians 6:10

Turn you to the strong hold, ye prisoners of hope: even to day do I declare that I will render double unto thee;

Zechariah 9:12

The only strength that is of any affect or value in the broken place is the strength that is of God. Natural strength is severed in any system that has experienced a breakage. When we try to exert influence, power or brute strength in a broken situation we are indulging in an exercise of futility.

I remember some years ago when I was still very much involved in athletic pursuit. I was participating in a staff vs. student's basketball game at a summer camp. In the midst of grappling for possession of the ball under the basket in an attempt to drive powerfully to the hoop I got pushed in the back. The intensity was so high that I was pushed into the wall behind the backboard. I raised my arms ahead of my body in a last ditch effort to brace for the inevitable impact. That was when I felt a snap and heard a pop. I became the running wounded that very moment with two fractured wrists. I continued to play not even realizing the damage that had been done due in part to my enthusiasm and the adrenaline coursing through my veins. However, as soon as I rested at the end of game both my wrists swelled immediately. Simple actions like waving or holding my backpack became difficult tasks almost instantaneously. It was like the strength in my arms was rendered invalid. Any strength that I did have stored in my arm muscles was coincidentally useless in aiding the activity of my arms because I had broken wrists.

How many of you know that your life can be like that too? If you are going through a season of brokenness, you may have latent strength but that strength is really ineffective because it is contained in a broken system. A powerful horse with a broken leg is a horse that is worthwhile only for the chopping block. The world system is broken. Therefore exercising of natural strength within the parameters and according to the principles and standards of this world will lead to hindered progress. This is because we are trying to operate in the fullness of our potential in faulty areas where we are not designed to function in anyway.

If my strength is therefore useless in the broken places, what strength do I have at my disposal? The Bible tells us that in the very things that bring me distress unto weakness for Jesus' sake are the very things in which I get instant strength.

Therefore I take pleasure in infirmities, in reproaches, in necessities, in persecutions, in distresses for Christ's sake: for when I am weak, then am I strong.

2 Corinthians 12:10

It also talks about the heroes of faith in the book of Hebrews who, "out of weakness were made strong, waxed valiant in fight."(Hebrew 11:34 partial) These scripture texts leads us to the conclusion that the only reason anyone is able to survive the broken place is because Jesus, the I AM, is in it with them. Daniel survived the lion's den because God was in it with him. The three Hebrew boys relaxed in the midst of the fiery furnace heated several times over because God was in it with them. The only way you can make it out of your dilemma of brokenness perfectly whole is if Jesus is in it with you. Paul survived persecution, imprisonment and oppression because God was in his suffering with him. But we must believe that if we were crucified with Him, and died with Him, then we shall arise with Him too. If we were overruled together, then we shall reign together with Him.

The "withness" of God neutralizes the "brokenness" of my will. Our Lord promised to be with us through thick or thin. In our suffering and even in sin God said He is with us. Therefore, this suggests that He is with us in our strength and in our weakness. Even more powerful than that is the fact that in our weakness His strength is what sustains us. These are great commendations to read about concerning God but they are commendations that depend on ones relationship with Jesus Christ. If you have no covenant with him He may be with you in your struggle and your sin but He will not intrude in your affairs unless provoked to do so by your faithful cry to Him. Jesus does not intervene where He is not invited.

Separation from God multiplies the pain that is evident in a struggle with brokenness. In our separation there is a severing of fellowship between God and us. Separation does not mean that God is unaware of our condition but rather it means that you have chosen to deny him access to your situation. He is everywhere, at all times waiting for an invitation into your situation.

Broken, *just to be made new*

The strength that I hold onto in the broken place is rooted in my knowledge of the fact that at the end of it all, I shall be made new. With newness comes a cleansing. There is a level of expectation that we have concerning new things. When we purchase a new car we expect to find a clean interior and exterior. We expect that the engine would be spectacularly polished. Although a brand new replacement of a broken item or relationship or possession is seldom the closest thing in mind on the occasion of an accident, incident or loss, one can agree that restoration is always a factor floating around in ones mind.

Can this possession be restored? Can the trust in that relationship ever be returned to where it was? These are the kinds of questions that are repeated in our moments of contemplation after experiencing loss due to brokenness. Many of us anticipate restoration but more of a patchwork outcome rather than a completely new makeover. Think about it. When we are at the latter end of a breakup, or taking inventory of an accident the usual practice is to replay the negative, and to consider what is lost. We seldom preview what good may be around the corner or what new things room has been made for. It could be a job, a car or a relationship. The first thought is to wonder if you could get another job that offered the same benefits and a matching salary. We say stuff like, "Will I be able to get another job in this field? This is the only field in which I am qualified!" Our expectations always lie in the arena of our present or latest circumstance.

Making career switches are intimidating prospects and usual residing in the recesses of our thoughts. The idea of doing something that is completely outside of one's experience but that one is capable of doing seems too foreboding. When it comes to a car we pay more attention to the insurance coverage to see what damage we could get repaired before we consider the possibility that this could be an opportunity to get something brand new.

With regard to relationships we mill over the pros and cons of the former relationship. Emotions run the gamut from sadness, to anger, to regret, to defensive advance. We make promises to ourselves that we will never fall for the dupe again and from hence we put every future suitor through a battery of test and acts of rejection until they basically are either repelled by us or begging us to be close. All the while we have settled to believe that we will never meet anyone who will fit our complete list of ideals, and this leads to an eventual mindset of settling and compromise for the first person who accumulates a relatively fair number of our list of ideals. The likelihood of one getting involved with someone totally new and the idea of beginning anew unconditionally almost never occur in our thought patterns. We figure that we know what we want, and if we were to go outside of what we are accustomed, it won't work.

And the vessel that he made of clay was marred in the hand of the potter: so he made it again another vessel, as seemed good to the potter to make it.

Jeremiah 18:4

The God that we worship is a God of newness. He is a God that relishes in the joy of making us anew. It is God's desire that his people walk in newness each and everyday.

We live in a world that goes through natural cycles of birth, death and rebirth. These are cycles of birth into new life, then maturity unto death that is followed by birth again into newness and the cycles continues again. When we walk with the mindset that any progress and maturation that we go through in this life is attached to a natural progression in God to a remaking into newness we will have a greater appreciation for the suffering that we go through. We will not only appreciate the suffering but we will grab on to the latent strength and power that is evident in the knowledge that even though I may feel helpless, God is working out the kinks. The fact that we are able to mentally process the experience of pain and recognize the pressure on our lives is evidence enough that the potter is at work in us.

How can I be strong in a broken place? I can only be strong in a broken place if I am strong in the Lord and in the power of His might. When I think of the idea of strength in a force that is separate from me I am often driven to the often intangibly nebulous idea of faith. It's one thing to profess that we have faith in God's strength to keep us but it's another to feel this faith in action. We speak faith but because of faith's spiritual nature we are never really sure if the object of our faith is real.

Faith can't be felt it must be believed. It must be believed, to have been fulfilled, in the spirit, once a statement of faith has been made. So it is herein where our greatest struggles with this walk lies. The idea of strength is a concept that is given its greatest credence in the physical but really possesses more value in the spiritual. Spiritual strength always outweighs physical strength. Physical strength may help you to walk away from a situation but if you don't have the physical wherewithal to retreat in a time of danger, your spiritual strength to resist is even greater than that needed to flee from that danger. Our strength in the broken place has to be in the God that controls and orchestrates the events of that broken experience.

A fine arts professor of mine in college made a statement once that left a profound impression on me. It was during a course in Basic Sculpture when we were discussing the great artisans of history and the professor said, "A great potter doesn't make a piece of pottery, but he discovers a piece in a clump of clay." As an art student I always felt myself somewhat out of the loop when it came to

Hugh J Harmon

such deep artistic observation because I just couldn't seem to conjure up any great images from the lumps of clay that I had to deal with. This professor in his explanation said that the pieces that the great sculptors created were not planned and prepped on paper but rather developed as the sculptor palmed the clay, and spun the wheel, and sprayed the water, and applied the pressure.

In the book of the prophet Jeremiah, God used the illustration of the potter and the clay and said that his relationship with his people can be at times be compared to the relationship of the potter to the clay. God is the potter and man is the clay. The clay as it sits on the spinning wheel moistened by the water and palmed by the potter is like the child of God as he or she sits on the spinning wheel of life moistened by the spiritual breath of God and palmed by his great hands. Does the clay have any strength in it of its own? No, it's strength to take shape and form a vessel that was of any use, was completely dependent on the manipulation of the hand of the potter. Do we have any strength to make ourselves vessels of honor unto God? I daresay, no. We need to depend on the powerful hand of God to shape us, and form us.

In the art of creating pottery the clay is put under great pressure. There is the pressure of the spinning wheel causing friction. There is the pressure of the water, helping to keep it moist but also wearing away the dry, stubborn outer layer of the clay. Then there is the pressure of the potters hands working to shape the clay contrary to its proclivity to form the shape of the motion it is experiencing. It is in this mixture of pressure that the broken place of this clay is gathering and harnessing strength. Good clay is able to go through all the pulls of pressure applied to it and still come out as a gloriously useful vessel. Even after all of this manipulation and pushing out of air and shaping and breaking down and reshaping again the clay still has to sit in the fiery furnace so that heat could be applied to it and its walls could be hardened. Again the strength that the finished clay pot has comes from without; it comes from the strength and the power of the fiery furnace. Can you be like the clay? Will you be willing to stand by and let the power, the strength and the might of the great potter shape you into the man and the woman that God desires for you to be?

Wherefore let them that suffer according to the will of God, commit the keeping of their souls to Him in well-doing, as unto a faithful Creator.
1 Peter 4:19

Wherefore let them that suffer—let them that are under pressure like clay suffer as according to the will of the Potter. In my season of suffering, in order to suffer in strength I must suffer with a knowledge that I am suffering according to the will of God. I am suffering in strength so that I may know Him and the power of His resurrection, and the fellowship of his sufferings, while being conformed to His death. The clay has to die to its former agenda. As a piece of clay all I had to do was sit in the corner of the workshop, all I had to do was to sit comfortably in a pile of mud. Clay is a type of mud. In our season of suffering we have to endure some dirty situations and places. Why, because God is building character, and He's out to get the glory in it all.

God puts us in the most unlikely places and situations, in areas where notoriety is more favored than fame, in places that are known more for the negative, than for the positive just to do a mighty work of transformation in us. We may be made to suffer in a shelter, in a group home, in a prison cell, in a burnt out crack house or even in the mental capsule of a bad decision. However, we must remember it's not because our lives are useless as the world would have us to believe. It is not even because we are so useful in our own right, but rather it is because it is in this place that God can show himself strong and show us how useless we are without his intervention. It is in our dire straits and with our lack of ability that God creates the perfect circumstances under which and through which He can show himself strong.

Jesus never estimated the value of his life according to the scenarios in which he was of the greatest use but rather he estimated the value of his life according to how much it lined up with the will of God. I'm not important because of my ability to do for God, but rather, because of the degree to which I am available for God to use me. Before God can use me, He must first make me useful. Before I can be of use to God I must be made to understand that my ability is useless to Him. Before God can use me He must mold me into a shape that is resilient enough for me to withstand the onslaught of the enemy.

God does not intentionally want you to feel pain, but he wants to build on your endurance and strength. Scientists studying the phenomenon of physical pain have come to the conclusion biologically that pain is weakness leaving the body. The stronger that you get the less pain that you feel in your place of struggle. The pain that you experience as a result of the struggle that you face is to build strength. It is to build resilience; it is to build stamina. The potter applies pressure to the piece of clay not just to massage it but rather to remove all the pockets of air that may be between the grains of clay. The pain that you feel as God squeezes the hot air out of your life is just part of your transition from weakness to strength. Pain is not the end all or be all, but rather it is a ways and a means to an end.

I remember in those pottery classes the series of experiences that the clay had to endure. The clay had to be manipulated as it spun on that wheel. Then we added water to prevent it from drying out. Next we squeezed it and kneaded it and bent it and broke it and beat it. This was all in the name of conforming the clay to the desired vessel. But even after the molding, bending, shaping and forming and even after my piece was made into the form that I desired, there still was one step. I realized that my finished piece was not really yet finished. It still lacked the beauty of the pieces that I saw lining the wall of the gallery. I saw that it lacked the polished look of the ones that lined the wall of the gallery. There was still the final step of trying the finished pottery in the potter's furnace, or the potter's oven. The piece had to be baked so that the form that it now had could be solidified.

After God has taken us through the valley. After the Spirit of God has taken us through the dry place to strip us of the things that essentially had us walking deformed lives, and immersed in dysfunctional behavior, he brings us to a place where we must be cemented in righteousness. This cementing in righteousness is done via that pressure and the purifying of fire. After you've been beaten, and bruised and bent into shape, and embarrassed in the name of Jesus Christ, you must then be tried in the fire. You must then be tried in the fire of resistance. This is a resistance that is designed to test the sturdiness of the foundation on which your renewed faith is built. It is a fire that not only tests the foundation of your faith but a fire that transforms your external appearance. The clay has to pass through the fiery furnace or the center of the oven so that its exterior could take on the finished look.

The fire applies to the clay vessel a great finish. Jesus Christ is the finisher. He is the potter and as we go through the fire we must understand that His hand is ever upon us. There are two times when the clay experiences fire. First, it is when the original vessel is broken. It has to be cast into the fire and melted so that a new vessel could be fashioned out of the recycled clay. The second time that clay experiences fire is when a new vessel has been fashioned out of clay and it has to be applied a finish. Fire is applied when you break it and fire is applied after you make it. Fire and thought of experiencing the intense heat and possibility of being burnt can be disconcerting but we must remember that the potter is always close by. In fact we can trust in the surety that the great potter throughout the process of making and remaking has his hands ever upon us. The potter must be always ready to pull the finished vessel from the fire just at the right time. Jesus is allowing some things to come upon you. He is allowing some circumstances to befall you that may appear to just burn you up. Those that you believed to be friends will burn you. Family members will do things and say things that will burn you but it will not kill you because God has his hands on you and He controls the fire.

> *Wherefore let them that suffer according to the will of God commit the keeping of their souls to him in well doing, as unto a faithful Creator.*
> **1 Peter 4:19**

As we suffer if we put our trust in the knowledge that Jesus Christ is in control, there is absolutely nothing to fear. If we dedicate our lives to do the things that line up with His revealed will for our lives, all will be well with our souls.

6.

Growing Pains

Confirming the souls of the disciples, and exhorting them to continue in the faith, and that we must through much tribulation enter into the kingdom of God.

Acts 14:22

Life is the continual experience of growth. Human life is the continual subjection of the body to development, maturation and growth due to the natural progression of life's cycles coupled with the effects of nature. Everything outside of our physical selves is designed in such a way as to exact upon us physical death. Life in its very nature creates friction, and friction causes a weakening in our composition.

Gravity, wind, water and the effects of the sun all work negatively against our physical bodies. The very things that we rely on to live, are the same things that speed up our disintegration. The sun gives us energy for life but the same sun causes my flesh to decay quicker if overexposed. Oxygen gives me breath for life but that same oxygen speeds up the decomposition of my cells. A warm touch gives me encouragement to live, but a warm touch actually causes superficial damage to the cells of the outer layer of my skin.

So we see that physical life from a truly simplified perspective is really the ability to balance ones physical interior with the natural exterior conditions of this world. Health is that balance and it is ruled by my ability to tip the scales sufficiently in favor of vitality on the inside. That is why we need to make sure that we are warm enough on the inside during the winter so as not to freeze to death. And then we have to keep cool enough on the inside during the summer so that we won't burn to death. What is God saying in these analogies of life? He is saying that in this life we will be in a few battles—they may be physical, mental or psychological but nevertheless it will be a battle, and in every battle there comes a degree of pain.

The Christian walk, the walk of spiritual growth that we must experience is a walk that comes with a degree of pain. And the pain that this walk brings is a pain that is directly attached to the growth that we experience in this walk. The walk is necessary, the growth is necessary and hence, the pain is necessary. That is a tough statement to accept as truth. And it takes on even greater gravity when we consider the level of pain that we have already experienced outside of this walk. How am I supposed to embrace salvation in Christ with the understanding that to walk with Him means pain? Why should I give God a chance? Why should I give God my life if I know that there is a portion of pain that I will still have to go through?

We come to church many times disillusioned with the world. We are in a season of discontent because the phase in our lives where worldly success had been our sustenance abruptly comes to an end. Sometimes it is in the fact that we are strung out on drugs and we finally get the revelation that what we've been subjecting our bodies too was totally destroying our lives. Other times it is within the prison cell feeling the cold hard wires of the bunk bed and staring at an uncertain future behind bars that we come to a realization that we need another chance. It may even be on a diagnosed deathbed in hospital after being told that we have a terminal illness that we come to the destiny decision that maybe just maybe God is the way to go. Then we come to church or we simply seek the counsel of a minister and we give our lives to God because we heard that when we do there is the promise of salvation from what we were going through. We read the Word and we hear that the truth shall make you free. We are prophesied to of the things that God has for us and the whole occasion is joyous. The people we meet and who testify of what God has done for them are all smiles and we can see that their life is truly better looking than ours. And we never really see the evidence of the pain that they had to go through on the way to their victory. Then you get saved and you begin to face the pain.

Little did you know that the enthusiasm that they were showing you was because you just joined the ranks of the soldiers of the Lord. You have become a soldier in a battle against the things of this world. That decision can cause great pain. The pain in the battle is not so much because of the strength of the enemy but rather is because of my flesh's past disposition as a part of the enemy's forces. We suffer in our transformation to a Christian walk because our minds, and our souls are accustomed to conforming to the world. Change is painful especially when we attempt to reposition ourselves out of a place that we have been in all our lives. Our spirit's desire to change but our flesh is unwilling to bend. This is where the breaking comes into play. After my mind has been motivated to follow God my soul has to be inspired to get in line. My mind wants to do right after hearing the Word but my flesh is still comfortable doing wrong. So this is why I have to experience pain because my flesh must be broken. The will of my flesh has to be broken.

God wants us to grow up in this walk. And that growth will bring pain. As recruited soldiers in the army of the Lord it is inevitable that we will experience pain. Since the fall of man there was no promise of comfort and ease but rather God desires us to grow up spiritually into a greater knowledge of Him, His Son and His Spirit. And that growth due to its separating of us from the world that we have grown accustomed too, causes us pain.

In the natural world there are great examples of experiential pain that comes with growth. In pregnancy a young lady who is due to give birth goes through a season of growth physically and mentally to deal with the developing child in her womb. As this child grows, the pain of conception in the mother grows. Without the pain there is a great chance that there is a degree of damage that has been sustained by the fetus. Many a miscarriage is physically painless and in that regard can cause great despair because the mother mistakes the lack of pain to be a sign of good progress. But when it comes to pregnancy pain is normal and should be expected. Pain in pregnancy indicates progress.

When a caterpillar goes through metamorphosis and changes to a cocoon and then eventually to a butterfly the experience of pain is necessary. The budding butterfly must experience pain because that very pain that it experiences as it pushes out of the cocoon is the same pain that imputes strength to its neophyte wings. An eagle as it breaks free of its egg feels pain that helps it to develop the muscles in its young wings. A young eagle that is pushed from its nest by its mother experiences the pain of separation but that pain is a necessary phase of life as it ultimately embarks on a life of flying solo. God wants to show us through the acts of nature how we can turn our pain into power. Without pain we would be unable to break the threshold that transforms pain into power.

Broken, *just to be made new*

Without pain we are unaware of the damage being done to our lives. As we deal with our season of brokenness and as we try to wrestle with the experience of pain we can come to a greater awareness of who we are. Our moments of pain in growth can tell us where we are weakest. If I don't feel any pain I won't have any clue of the mess that I am making of my life. Emotional pain alerts us to the mistakes we've made in relationships in our life. This is the type of pain that we love to ignore. Samson must have felt great emotional pain having succumbed to the deception of Delilah and that pain was a constant reminder in his time of service as a prisoner to the Philistines. However, he used that pain to garner enough courage and fortitude to seek God once again to deal his enemies a greater defeat than he had done in his physical prime.

Mental pain alerts us to the bad decisions that we have made in our lives. Regret, doubt, discouragement and shame are all the catch phrases that accompany poor decisions. David experienced mental pain in the aftermath of his contrived encounter with Bathsheba. They had a child as a result of blatant infidelity on David's part. She had the child but the child had to die because of the evil that surrounded its conception. Many of us are in a place of regret, and shame because of the mental pain that we are experiencing due to dysfunctional decisions. Physical pain alerts us to the cuts, bruises and scars that we have suffered in life. The woman with the issue of blood was aware of her condition because there was pain in her life. Without the pain she was suffering, and without the issue of blood she may have died and may have never been aware of the fact that she was dying. And the moment that her pain ceased she was aware of the fact that she was healed.

Pain that is present keeps me seeking a remedy. While pain that is past informs me that I'm healed. Without the pain of abuse we won't know that we need a new relationship. Without the pain of a guilty conscience we won't know that we did wrong. Without the pain of that headache we won't know that we have developed a tumor. Without pain we would be dying without knowing it.

Growing up my track coach used to always say, "Pain is a sign of weakness!" If I had a back pain he would say it was because m stomach muscles were weak. If I had stomach pain he would say that meant that my thigh muscles were weak. If I had a hamstring pain he would say that meant that my calf muscles were weak. I was led to believe that pain relief lay only in gaining strength. We have to understand that without pain in our lives we would have no indicator of growth, or of the places where we are weak. In addition, we have to believe that without pain in our lives there will be no opportunity to experience the blessing of relief.

The Bible says that our Lord forgives all our iniquities, and heals all our diseases. It also says, "He sent His Word and healed them, and delivered them from their destruction." The Bible also says that He is our deliverer, our redeemer and our comfort. Paul in his epistle to the church at Corinth said, "Blessed be the God and father of our Lord Jesus Christ, the Father of mercies and God of all comfort." If the Bible promises all of this relief from pain that means I must sometime in this walk face some pain of illness, some form of trouble from which I must be delivered and some place of discomfort, doubt or discouragement that I must be comforted in.

The world says no pain, no gain and God says without pain there is no growth. Growth in God is to accept that as we walk with Him, we must suffer with Him.

Think it not strange concerning the fiery trial which is to try you, as though some strange thing happened to you; but rejoice to the extent that you partake of Christ's sufferings.

1 Peter 4:12-16

Broken, *just to be made new*

To gain the blessing of a new birth we must endure pain. In Genesis 37 we see the pain that Joseph had to endure. He had to deal with betrayal by his brothers. He had to endure the false accusations by his boss's wife. But it was all in order to fulfill the promises spoken over his life. Joseph had to endure pain that resulted in his elevation to a place of authority even in a foreign land. Moses had to go through the pain of separation from his kin at birth. He had to deal with the rejection of his own people and self-imposed exile in the wilderness. He even had to face intimidation from Pharaoh in order to gain God's election, Israel's freedom and God's blessing. David had to go through the pain of loving someone who hated him, and living on the run from one whom he greatly respected. But it was all in order that he might gain the respect of God, have the power to stand as a great ruler and the fortitude to be king over God's people.

7.

Ready to die?

For he that is dead is freed from sin.
Romans 6:7

Are you ready to die? The question pierced my conscience. Was I ready to die just to be a part of this? It was all attractive up and appeared to be "all good" until he asked that question. And not wanting to come across as some punk I quickly replied, "I'm ready!" And wasn't that the farthest from the truth. The process of indoctrination up to this point was palatable but when this big brother made this query all my thoughts went to the horror stories I had heard about from fraternal folklore. I had heard stories of other young men who had inadvertently lost their lives going through the intake process to be a part of one of these brotherhoods. I was now potentially setting myself up to become a part of that history. I said that I was ready to die but my understanding of what acceptance of death meant was far from reality.

I am alive today and that is an assurance that I survived that possibility. But how many of us if faced with that question from a spiritual perspective could clearly and boldly reply in the affirmative.

Today I can securely say that I am not afraid to die, because I know that at the end of it all, I shall live again. I am convinced of the victorious promise of everlasting life that comes with salvation. I am also convinced that fulfillment in life is but a single decision or a single shout away for each and every one of us. Have you ever been in a place where you felt that you were over a thing? You had determined in your spirit that you had locked this thought, this habit, or this behavior away in your past. You went a week, a month, three months, then half a year and then even a few years and then a new year rolls in, and you find yourself revisiting those once retired thoughts. Guess what? You have a problem and your problem is that you have yet to cross the bridge of deliverance.

Having developed the discipline to avoid a thing for a long period of time does not guarantee that you have been permanently delivered from a thing. Some of us want to come out of the things that we were into by stealth rather than by death. Closing ones eyes and spinning around twice does not equal sure separation from a thing. Many of us are willing to forget a habit or a certain type of behavior for a while but we are afraid of the permanence that comes with dying to our soulish desires and will. We rather stick old skeletons in the closet in the attic rather than throw them out in the garbage. This is because we have an inert desire and need to revisit these habits and adore them even if from a distance because all that we need is a close proximity to these skeletons to reawaken and fulfill the once hidden desire in us.

Why aren't we over it yet? Why do we still fall? The problem is that we have not come to understand that if we aren't fighting in this walk then we are inevitably falling. In this world, our victory is assured once we continue to fight, the moment we rest on our laurels we will fall. Falling takes no effort, but fighting even to the death takes energy.

When I think of the idea of the internal and the outward struggle that we as Christians face living in a world of contradictions as we do, I am drawn to the analogy of crossing a bridge. I'm led to refer back to my first book when I spoke on the work of Jesus Christ in reconciling us back to God. In that book I delved into the thought of God through Jesus bridging the gap between himself and fallen man. The problem isn't today that we don't have a way to get back to God and to get our lives in order. Rather, the problem is that we are hesitant or callous in using the way as prescribed by God himself.

Many of us have come to the bridge and we are afraid to cross it. Some of us have come to the bridge, and the bridge is the cross and for a myriad of reasons we fear going beyond the cross. Salvation; the free gift we receive at the cross gets us pass the toll booth with the toll paid, with the ransom paid by the blood, but we have to learn how to move beyond reception of salvation.

There are three types of folk being referred to here. Those who have heard the word of salvation, they have approached the cross in curiosity and they have seen the pain that was suffered there but they still believe that what they did could not possibly be covered or wiped clean by the act of Jesus' surrender to the cross. These are the people who come to church and they enjoy the atmosphere, the company of believers is encouraging but they never make a decision for Christ because they truly believe themselves unworthy. They may actually believe that God will set himself upon them sooner or later and they would never have to openly confess their need for Him.

Then there are those who make a decision with zeal. Many times they have had some tragedy in their lives, some event that radically transforms their attitude toward life. However, after making a decision for Christ and after the initial anxiety wears off and they are faced with demonically assigned opposition and temptation they fall. They also may simply resort to past practices unable to trust in the latent power that comes with spiritual maturity and an ongoing connection with God. For these people the idea of the supernatural, omnipotent attributes of God are incomprehensible and beyond their normal train of thought. They can't think beyond their past experience of God, or of what they thought God to be. God has been inevitably boxed into their definition of somewhat limited extraordinary provision and ability.

The third type of person believes God, and believes in the finished work of the cross. They thrust their every need and want at the foot of the cross, and they walk away not backward into what they are used to but forward into the unknown beyond the cross. They go to that place and they tarry for the next promise to be fulfilled. They wait with anticipation for Jesus to take them to another level so that they could experience the more that He promised to give in this new abundant life. They walk not with any clear-cut expectations but more with a naïve acceptance that God is in control of all circumstances what looks good and what seemingly looks bad it didn't matter.

God wants his people to be in the party of the third person. We have to walk just far enough to pass salvation, unto the planks of redemption and then make our footprints step into the realm of deliverance and sanctification. But in order for this to happen we must be willing and able, and ready to die. In dying we are broken, and in being broken we

77

are now subject to the process of remaking. The greatest hindrance to the advancement of the kingdom to the place of manifest glory is the wholesale act o decision making for Christ but indecision about crossing the bridge.

Again I ask are you ready to die? Are you afraid of death? I am not afraid to die, because I know that at the end of it all, I'll live. But I did not always have that attitude, and that sure of a feeling concerning this walk in salvation. My strong sentiments came after a season of study and experience of the grace and mercy of God working some things out in my life. I had to transition from a place of being sure about my decision to follow Christ and from being unsure about my ability to live according to his statutes. And from there, I had to move to a place where I now understand that my ability to live according to his will is not predicated on my personal skill at living right but on Jesus' substitutionary act of living righteously through me.

Our lack of readiness to die is due to a misinterpretation of what it means to die. We have grown to fall in love with life regardless of how screwed up it may be, and death has become a foreign feeling or experience. But what really is death, is it as final and scary as the world has portrayed it to be. The gravity with which the world handles the event of death speaks volumes. The dread with which we approach even the topic in our conversation tells that it is something that we wish to passionately avoid. But when we look at death the way that God would like us to look at death we come to a new revelation of what it really entails.

When we come to the cross and seek the application of His blood to our lives, we must understand that we are actually choosing to die with Jesus. That seems hard to swallow. Why do I have to die with Christ in order to experience salvation? The type of death that I am referring to is the death that is a separation from the things of the world that once brought you life. When we starve our souls of the emotional triggers that once bathed our consciences we actually deal a deathblow to our will. This death is our breaking. Are you willing to break away from that old habit? Are you willing to break away from that old secret sin or that sin causing weight that has so easily belayed your thought life? When you say, yes to these questions then and only then can God safely break you so that he could pour you out and make you anew.

What is your story? Is it one of wondering into church after a night of boozing, smoking, drugging and sexing? Are you the one filled with guilt, and sitting in the presence of the preacher who just proclaimed the goodness of the Lord? This preacher speaks of the faithfulness of God. He speaks about how God even while you're still in sin died on your behalf. He speaks of the last and evil days. And you sit there finding it hard to believe in all the doom and gloom that he is painting in his sermon coupled with the promises of peace if you would just accept Jesus. There is the weeping and the gnashing of teeth and the separation of the goats and the sheep. Then there is the finality of the men and women being cast into the lake of fire. It is then capped off with the reminder of eternal torment that awaits those who don't believe. Are you the man or the woman that consequently runs to the altar guilty, ashamed and scared? I'll be honest with you I have been that person at least a few times and unfortunately my motivation was one of fear. God doesn't want a decision motivated by fear because that decision will remain just that a decision that lacks any decisive action. Fear is not a powerful enough force to overcome soulish desire. This is why we must choose to die to the things that are binding us to this world and not just temporarily run away from them.

We walk in newness when we surrender to death in Christ. Christ died and he rose again, and if I attach what little life I have right now to Him, I will die with Him and arise with Him. If it is that easy why don't we do it? Our flesh many times over rules our spirit. The flesh is too accustomed to being fulfilled and the spiritual side of us suffers from neglect. Having lived much of our lives revolving around the idea of appetizing our flesh the thought of allowing our spirits a transfusion of power is secondary. For most of our lives we lived to eat, drink and be merry. We lived to belong to the in-crowd. We did the things that made us feel good. We did the things that brought physical pleasure but left us in mental torment.

We knew that smoking potentially damaged our lungs but it felt good. We knew that sex with multiple partners and out of wedlock was both sinful and harmful to our health but it felt good. We knew that eating too much fatty, salty, sweet or fried foods was not good but it felt good to us. We knew that selling drugs to mothers, fathers, sons and daughters could greatly destroy the fabric of family and potentially plunge neighborhoods in chaos but it felt good to have a fist full of dollars. We knew that prostituting what was precious to us to persons who were little more than strangers all in the name of loneliness and unmet needs was less than noble but it felt good never having to commit to love just one.

Newness is fully experienced when we adjust our understanding of what is meant by death in Christ. Our view of death is physical expiration. It is a view of death as defeat, sadness, darkness and derision. We see death in Christ as acceptance of some deflated joy. We too often associate this death as a ceasing of life. Skewed interpretations of the Christian world-view have led to postulations about death in Christ being an acceptance of the world's contradictions. It says that if life outside of Christ is joyous, death in Christ is sadness, absent of joy. It also says that if life outside of Christ is wealth, death in Christ is poverty and need. Lastly it says that if life outside of Christ is one of fame and fortune, death in Christ is to be assigned a season of struggle, suffering and surviving misfortune. Christians and seekers alike have been taught that lack, less than enough with contentment or just enough constitutes ones degree of closeness to Christ.

Death in Christ must begin in a place of recognizing what we have to die to. What are you willing to let God break inside of you?

How shall we, that are dead to sin, live any longer therein?
Romans 6:2

Our death is a death to sin, to the practice of it, and the compulsion to do it. It is also a surrender of our will. In death we lose control of our choices and decisions. To die in Christ is to give up control to a faithful God. My will is to seek after fame, fortune and friends. However, God's will is for me to be separated, set apart, to be made Holy and acceptable unto Him. My will is to please the masses, and to gain popular appeal. But God's will is for me to spread an unpopular Gospel, to promote and practice an unpopular standard and to question the status quo. Death in Christ is to act only according to the mandates of God, therefore death in Christ is to submit to prayer and communion with God. It is the act of moving only when God moves.

Death in Christ is to render the former things null and void in your life. The former abuses must be curtailed and not revisited. The former lack, the former need and the former curses must cease with your generation. The former habits and the former immoral relationships all must be put to rest. When Jesus hung on the cross he said, "It is finished..." and that meant that the former convictions spoken over his people were finished. The price was paid, never to be paid again. The commodity was removed from the market once and for all. I am no longer for sale because God said take him off of the shelf. Take him and break him so that I can make him new.

Hugh J Harmon

8.

You are not your own, God's still doing something with you...

For ye are bought with a price: therefore glorify God in your body, and in your spirit, which are God's.

1 Corinthians 6:20

Many of us live with the concept that we exist in "a world within a world." We strive to carve out our own comfortable spaces, and places in society. We seek the finances, the careers, the ends, and the relationships, the possessions and trophies that would make us comfortable. We seek to ensure our joy and our own peace of mind. Unfortunately, many of us seek these comforts, although not deliberately, but inextricably at the expense of making others uncomfortable. These are all noble pursuits, desiring to place oneself above the fray apart from life's setbacks and seemingly chronic constraints and assuring one's families economic security in this time of uncertainties. However, these pursuits soon fall effortlessly back down to earth or metaphorically lose air when we go after them absent from any spiritual considerations. We must be constantly made aware of the spiritual facet to our lives. We must not only understand that we are spirit beings but we must also

83

understand that we are revived spirit beings who exist on the life support of a risen savior. Your life is not your own. My life is not my own.

How can this be? How is it that we live in this world in seemingly effortless dependence on our own strength and by our own decisions but yet still I could be driven to proclaim that the life that we have been living apart from God's counsel is not our own? The Bible says in the scripture text that opens this chapter that we were bought with a price. An actually previous to this declaration by the author of this epistle to the church at Corinth, we have another even more direct rhetorical statement. Paul the apostle given credit for penning this text of scripture asks, "Know ye not that your body is the temple of the Holy Spirit, which is in you...?" Who does this refer to? Can I stand on this word even if I have lived most of my life denying Jesus' lordship over my life? This text does speak to a church at Corinth. It speaks to a body of believers. It speaks to a group of men and women who have given their lives over to God. But does it also speak to the man or the woman who is presently walking in sin? Does it speak to the man or the woman who has yet to proclaim Jesus Christ as Lord? Does it speak to the man or the woman who has expressly said that they do not believe in the lordship of Jesus Christ?

The question when we really think about it is does God extend this statement of purpose to all men or is it a word extended only to those who have confessed their belief in Christ? When we examine the context and the pretext of the scripture we are directly led to conclude that this was a message specifically to a believing congregation. However, when we align the text with other scripture concerning the mission and the purpose of Christ we must truly consider that this was a Word for all men.

But God commendeth his love toward us, in that, while we were yet sinners, Christ died for us.

Romans 5:8

84

The Bible does say that while we lived in sin God died for us. The thing that separates the saint from the sinner in this text is that the saint is justified through faith while the sinner is yet waiting for their justification to be wrought through their acclimation to a place of faith.

Therefore, it precludes us to remind friends and family members who are living outside of the body of believers that despite their denial they still live at the behest of a graceful God who chooses daily to extend their lives even though they live apart from him. They may live apart from his direction but they don't live apart from his influence. And even in their separation from his direction they still have to circumnavigate their lives subject to the mandates that He has set in place. There is no place that we could go that will render us far enough away from God to make his influence in our lives limited. And this is because God is an all-encompassing being that works by any morally legitimate means necessary to assure the advance of his will. If the world within a world in which you live is a world devoid of Jesus Christ that does not mean that it is a world unsubdued by his power.

The devil will have us to believe that we have ultimate power over our lives. He would have us to believe that we have no need for God. In fact, he really wants us to fall into the same trap that he fell into when he declared his "I wills..." and was cast out of heaven. He wants us to begin to believe that we are in ourselves gods. He wants us to adopt the attitude that if we were to attain a high enough level of intellect and bank of knowledge of ourselves we will consequently develop some lack of necessity of having a God to trust and believe in. However, having an attitude or adopting a mindset or even accepting a belief system does not mean that we have finally gotten it right. In fact many times our attitudes, mindset and beliefs are all wrong despite the conviction that is attached to them. However, the Lord puts us into situations and difficult circumstances or even allows seemingly simply solved problems to chronically plague us just to bring us to a place of identifying our need for him. Our lives need Christ in it. Our lives need a place and a point of breaking when we see that God is doing something in us, by us, through us and for us. Only then can we truly accept the reality of God making us new through the manipulation of our mess.

Another way that we promote the attitude of selfish advance versus selfless sharing of our resources and ourselves is in the way that we relish and we obsess over our privacy. Privacy in our affairs is of utmost importance to us. We cover our lives in secrecy believing that in privacy we can keep trouble from entering our lives. We speak softly and in the dark, believing that if men can't hear us, God surely can't hear us either. We operate in the comfort of shadows doing our dirt and believing that if we walk circumspectly in the light, that our sins done in the dark will stay hidden. But privacy, my friend, is essentially an act of covering. It is an act of hiding. It is the attitude of turning off the lights in the middle of an argument and believing that the darkness would solve the dispute. This is how many of us deal with the struggles and the problems that we face in an effort to keep them hidden from society. We turn out the lights by closing our eyes and covering our ears and we believe that if we just wait a little while and open our eyes slowly and unplug our ears slowly the whole affair would disappear. In fact, it may create a momentary state of confusion and actually escalate the dysfunction—elevating the argument and making the problem even more disruptive to your state of being.

Jesus reminded us in the Sermon on the Mount that the *Father seeth in secret.* Paul tells us in the epistle to the church at Rome that *God will judge the secrets of men.* Our lives should be a walk in which we ask God to cleanse us from our secret faults. Striving for secrecy and exclusivity in the experience of the affairs of our lives is to strive to live with a constant veil that obscures us from the world's view. God never endorsed us living in a bubble outside of the gaze or the affects of the world. God actually wants our lives to be open books from which the world can read of what it is to trust in Him. He has a master plan that may have an impact on your life, my life and on our lives collectively without our permission. The plan of God far exceeds any individually based agenda we may have.

Abundant life is impossible if we don't live with a full understanding that our body and our strength is given vitality only when we live in an intimate relationship with a holy God. I cannot live abundantly satisfied unless I live within his grace. I cannot live satisfied unless I live according to His word. Satisfaction in my life is not achieved by my work to be like Christ but is achieved by my availability in allowing Christ to become a part of my life. Jesus said abide in me and I in you. Abide here is derived from the Greek word *meno* which means to stay in a given place, or a given state. Jesus desires that we remain in relationship that we stay in a state of expectancy. It means to tarry, or to remain in the presence of. The Bible also says that He that dwells in the secret place of the Most High shall abide in the shadow of the Almighty. Abide here comes from the Hebrew word, *liya* which literally means to stop over night; it means to lodge all night, to tarry or continue all night. The implication is that especially and even in our darkest hour we must stand, stop or lodge in Jesus.

The six degrees, more or less, that separate us in this life, be it at our times of denial of our need for Jesus, or after our acceptance of His place in our lives, are still interconnected by the will of God. Our lives messed up or made up by seemingly independent decisions on our part are still subject to the ultimate will of God. It is due to his grace and his mercy that we are able to even disobey Him. And it is by his grace and mercy that He works to orchestrate the outcome of his will for our lives and the lives of those connected to us. The blood of Christ sanctifies us in order that we may be placed into lock step with the plan of God. Our sanctification that involves an initial stage of breaking is ultimately a divine separation. It is a setting apart. It is a set up that due to the limited scope of our natural vision appears to be a setback. When we enter into sanctification we shift from the natural to a complete dependence on the unseen supernatural. We move from comfortability to discomfort, and even to a place of unfamiliarity. In real sanctification low expectations are displaced by high expectations. In sanctification we move from a known location—familiar friends, relationships, habits, and practices to a place that we have never been in before.

When we feel most inept and unable to direct our lives is when we have actually gotten to a place where we could truly secure the direction of our lives. This is because our ineptness or our inability is a signal that we are now truly available for God to do something great and transforming in our lives. Men and women who are driven always seemingly contemplating the next move, dotting Is and crossing T's, living like control freaks unable to let go of the minute detail of their lives are people who usually have no time for an intrusive God. We worship an intrusive God. He is a God that is concerned even about the smallest details of our lives but he can't get to put his hands upon those issues if we are constantly meddling in the pot.

Life is like a puzzle and God's plan is to complete the assembly of this puzzle. We are the pieces and the people that we encounter in our lives are the pieces that were designed to connect neatly with us. God is separating the pieces of the puzzle according to the shapes of the edges. He is also separating the pieces according to color. God in his infinite wisdom has the final finished picture ever before Him in his thoughts. Therefore it is a simple process for him to arrange the pieces so that they match the picture. You and I

Broken, *just to be made new*

are the pieces that he has set to the side. God has set us to the side as he puts the other pieces of our lives together. Some of us are on the way out of our brokenness and God is working on the hearts and minds of those connected to us so that when we do come out all that we have desired from those people closest to us, would be available to us. God is working out family problems, and he is even moving negative influences out of our way, so that we could take our rightful place. Think about it, would God bring you this far to then let you sit and see every dream and promise spoken into your spirit walk away from you? God desires patience on our parts. He desires patience as He moves your case to the top of the pile. He desires patience as he moves your resume to the front of the filing cabinet. He is moving on the hearts of wives, husbands and kids so that when you come back to them they would be able to see His hand on your life. He requires your patience as he puts the other pieces to your puzzle together.

In our season of brokenness God is saying the rut that you are in right now is temporary. All He needs for us to do is wait patiently. God requires patient endurance. Endurance is not only the ability to wait but it is the ability to wait while experiencing resistance. Our endurance is built not by merely waiting in effortless ease but rather is achieved by surviving the struggle, and dealing with the pain.

> *Count it all joy when you fall into various trials, knowing that the testing of your faith produces patience. But let patience have its perfect work, that you may be perfect and complete, lacking nothing.*
>
> **James 1:2**

Our knowledge of God begins with our fear of God. And our fear of God begins with our experience of His power. As I suffer with Him I come to an understanding of the power He possessed to endure the things that He did on behalf of an entire world of sinners. To be used by God requires first the act of being made useful by God—through our immersion in the trials of life that render us useless especially to ourselves. Unfortunately we strive to be useful in our own eyes and we in turn misuse the talents and gifts that we have been divinely equipped with. This in turn renders us truly useless to God in the advancing of His will here on earth.

As long as we could keep in our minds and our hearts the idea that what we go through and experience in this life ultimately is not only meant for our sole benefit. But also is for the benefit of everyone assigned to be influenced by us, we will stay grounded and at God's disposal. God's plan is so great and so forward thinking that there have been souls assigned to us that will be in our lives simply to witness the goodness of God on our lives.

9.

You're not forgotten, you're not forsaken. God's just shakin' things up in you

Come and let us return to the Lord, for He has torn so that He may heal us; He has stricken so that He may bind us up.

Hosea 6:1(Amplified)

As I sit down to write this chapter I have the distinct heartfelt desire to stoke a fire of revival in all that will have the opportunity to read it. This is due in part to a period of struggle that I have been personally going through, and a word of encouragement that I recently received and drove me to study the idea of God using the restricting events of our natural lives to free our spiritual selves. For me personally the last few years have been a time of almost chronic worry about unfulfilled aspirations, but this one word was like a chemotherapy cure that shot straight through my spirit and neutralized these worries. Have you ever gotten a simple word from a preacher or from a friend or even from a stranger that seemed to bare a resolute power about it as if it were spoken from God directly through this person to you? This word bore the very breath of God, and I pray that it will bear the same power as I attempt to deliver it to you.

Hugh J Harmon

At the opening of the New Year, January 1st, 2006 while seated in the sanctuary at my home church, Love Fellowship Tabernacle, the Kingdom Church in Brooklyn, New York, I received a revelatory word. It was approximately a few seconds before the clock struck twelve, and the midnight mass worship service was in full swing. After taking a quick glance at his watch my pastor, Overseer Hezekiah Walker turned to the congregation with the microphone held to his lips and made a prophetic declaration that has since lit a fire of personal revival in my life. Pastor Walker said, "This 2006 is the year of increase!" A shout went up that filled the sanctuary and resounded throughout that Brooklyn neighborhood. It must have caused some unrest among our neighbors and may have even created some disgruntled responses but even more so it caused unrest in my spirit. It wasn't so much the reaction of the collective body of saints as it was the small still whisper that I heard echoed behind it in my spiritual ears, and that word was, "This is the year of your coming out!" God was giving me a personal pep talk. He was telling me that any increase that I hoped to experience that year was predicated on my taking steps to come out of the rut.

Too long I had been hearing about the turnaround and believing that I was counted among those who would have a turnaround but I never actually did anything to affect that turn. Today, regardless of the time of the year or the year in which you are reading this chapter, I've come to tell you, "This is it! This is the year that you have been waiting for! This is the year of your coming out!" I want you to understand the power behind that declaration. For when you declare it into the atmosphere that this is the year that you will be coming out and you purpose in your heart to take the first step you are actually speaking back to God His expressed will for your life. Before you go any further I need you to repeat this to yourself, *This is the year of my coming out, in Jesus name!*

92

Broken, *just to be made new*

Many of us due to unfocused beginnings and relatively late entry into the life of salvation look at our lives and we are many times filled with great regret. We have regret about the things that we have allowed to aimlessly develop and ultimately become a source of debilitating opposition to our experience of the abundant life in Christ. We also regret the time that we wasted indulging in the unprofitable joys of this world. Maybe it was immaturity, callous financial mismanagement that has led to us having disparate economic status—living from paycheck to paycheck, or not having enough check for the bills that we have incurred. Or maybe it was simple procrastination when it came to pursuing the completion of our education, or a lack of input into the sustenance of a marriage relationship, whatever the case may have been, we get into place where we are riddled with guilt and regret.

Regret is the enemy of expectation. Anytime we allow regret to linger expectation is encumbered and prevented from attaining its rightful place of governance in our lives. Our lives can only get better if we think better of ourselves. When we have expectations we create a vehicle upon which our desires may travel. This travel will either be in the form of great steps ahead of where we currently stand, or can be the minor act of inching along in life. Therefore, expectation must be prefixed with greatness. We must possess and foster great expectation, and there is no one that has greater expectations of us than God himself does.

For I know the thoughts that I think toward you, saith the Lord, thoughts of peace, and not of evil, to give you an expected end.
Jeremiah 29:11

As a human being existing in a fallen world our lives are betwixt and between a paradigm. The enemy of our soul is out to get rid of us and God is out to restore us. The Bible says that the devil is the thief, and he the thief comes to steal, kill and destroy. There is no positive outcome that is purposed in the devils desire to connect with us. He is not

93

interested in prospering us. He is more interested in formulating our demise. But God,...once again we hear the resolute conjunction of change, but...God. The devil may be up to no good, but God is out for your good. These constantly opposing forces working on our lives can create more confusion than confidence in us especially if we walk unfocused.

God would love to change it so that our lives lean more towards an equilibrium, where the pendulum swings to a greater degree on the side of God's will for our lives versus the devils will for our death. God will never supersede our inner desire just to bring us onto Him. But He will use the predicaments of our lives to cause us to come to a place where we understand that we need His intervention.

God orchestrated the place that you are in right now, both physically and mentally. This may seem like a difficult pill to swallow. How could it be that God wants this for me? It isn't that God wants it for us but rather it is that he wants us to choose. And unfortunately we ignorantly, and more often than necessary, choose the path of least resistance, which is usually the path to destruction--the path that takes the least effort on our part. God is then forced to work with what we give him, and what we give him many times isn't much. We wonder why God didn't deliver us from poverty before but who is the one really to blame? God didn't make those ill-fated decisions to spend without considering future expense, we did. We wonder why we had to go through the things we went through early on in life. However, we fail to consider that most of the time there was a warning or a way of escape presented to us that we ignored because of the temporary success that our decisions brought, success that lacked significance.

The breaking that we experience in Christ is relative to the degree of our separation from Him. The further you are away from his will the greater will be the need of and the severity of your breaking. The more messed up you are the greater reshaping God has to do in your life. We fail to see the necessity of discipline even in the progression of our walk with Christ. We see salvation and deliverance in Christ to be an instantaneous work that little depends on learning a process. This is where many have failed and have begun to doubt the veracity of God's word. Our conception of Christ and what He will and can do in our lives is convoluted and unclear. This is due to the fact that little attention is given to the teaching that God can do for us only what we allow him to do. And we are only able to allow him to do if we are disciplined in the mores of righteousness. Most of us have lived a greater portion of our lives in sin; practicing sin and well versed in the disciplines of sin and then we expect our soulish will to automatically adopt a code of righteousness. This must be taught. Spiritual disciplines must be inculcated into our lives over time through study of the word, prayer in his will and fasting with an open ear for his voice.

As you stand in your brokenness, realize the length of time that you stay in it depends on your ability to adopt spiritual discipline. It might look and feel like you are in hell right now. But we must remember that our human sight and our feelings are unreliable instruments against which to measure the level of our transforming condition. The enemy wants us to concentrate on what we are going through, while losing sight of where and what we are going to. The experience that we are in right now is really a false hell. It is a false hell created by the devil to kill us but used by God to create in us an appreciation for the real heaven. Some of us had to go through what we went through because if God had delivered us any earlier we would never have come to the revelation that we needed Him. Some of us did not really have to go through what we went through. However, when God spoke we ignored Him. God spoke and we ran the other way. God spoke and we told him not now. Nevertheless, He didn't get you here to kill you; he got you here to save you.

This is the year of your coming out. And it begins with you seeing your life the way God sees it, and that vision then should lead you to want to change. The want or the desire for change must then translate to an active pursuit of knowledge and wisdom concerning the disciplines of righteousness. Only when we are adequately equipped will we be ready to reenter the battle. This life is a battlefield and those unequipped to deal with opposition, and temptation, are soon swallowed up. At what level are you? Are you a cadet—newly entered and initiated into basic training? Or are you a seasoned infantryman, adequately prepared to deal with the accouterments of war?

There is security that we can lay hold to in our brokenness when we realize that our recovery is God ordained. God has no evil intention toward us. Despite all that we've done, all that we've said, and all the bad decisions that we may have made, we live subject to a God that is faithful. He is a God that is gracious and a God that is merciful. We worship a God that would have it that all would be saved but due to man's freedom to choose otherwise, all men will not be saved. Nevertheless, mercy and grace are extended toward us with each new day. Every new day that you are allowed to breathe the breath of life is another day that God gives us an opportunity to choose him. As a new day breaks in our lives and the sun peaks over the horizon God is extending a fingertip of life abundantly in him again. He has been taking you through a season of brokenness and has taken the time to preserve the very parts of you that make you uniquely you. He is ready to make you anew and have you to walk in the newness of life but first he requires that you possess a transformed mind. A broken spirit remade can be either a spirit that holds a grudge or it can be a spirit that gives every new relationship a clean slate to work with. God hasn't forgotten you and he certainly hasn't forsaken you. He's simply trying to shake some sense into you.

Broken, *just to be made new*

Thou art a God ready to pardon, gracious and merciful, slow to anger and of great kindness, a God that forsakest not.
Nehemiah 9:17

Last night you were crying because of the dissolved relationship, or the ruptured friendship. But today you feel the peace and joy that the Lord promised would come in the morning. The Bible says that joy of the Lord is my strength. It says that weeping may endure for a night but joy comes in the morning. What's to come is better than what's been. The best of your yesterday in the world can't compare to the better of your tomorrow in God. Your latter end shall be greater if you take advantage of the loss that God wrought in your life. Some of the things that you lost you lost them for your own good. Don't hang on to them in regret. Thank God that you had the experience of knowing them but take it as a lesson and move on.

There is a kingdom blessing promised to us if we would just hold on. As God works out the kinks in our lives, and as he takes us through the valleys and dark places to release us from some things that held us in our times of safety, we must trust in the fact that we are still in his hands. There are no safer places in this world than in his hands or in his will. Before salvation God has his hands on our lives. After salvation God has us in his hands.

Regardless of the resistance, trial and tribulation that we may face know that the things we lose are meant to be lost in the fire. Many of the things that afflict us are driven out of our lives in our seasons of distress. This is because we often begin to prioritize our lives when we encounter chronic pain. Someone who is suffering from a chronic illness is better able to determine what is important to them and their well-being than someone who is in perfect health. Illness and affliction can sometimes open our eyes to those things that are useless to our survival.

Hugh J Harmon

Sometimes the places in which we face our greatest fears are the places where we lose those that are of a greatest hindrance to our coming out. Some of the people intimately related and connected to us fortunately separate in those times when we are under greatest persecution. At those times we look at the loss and we sympathize with the friend that deserts us because we don't want someone else to go through what we are going through simply because of there association with us. However, the breakup might be the best thing for us. This is because many times those intimately tied to us can negatively persuade us to settle for the place that we are in. They believe that they are speaking and acting with your best interest at heart, but their small-mindedness is actually a subconscious attempt to punctuate your life before God is finished with you.

Behold, at that time I will undo all that afflict thee: and I will save her that halteth, and gather her that was driven out; and I will get them praise and fame in every land where they have been put to shame.
Zephaniah 3:19

At that time, at what time, at the time of your coming out, God will deal with all that encumbered you. He will deal with all that has been a hindrance. He will deal with all that oppressed you. Everyone and everything that has ever hindered you from connecting with God, shall be reformed or it shall be destroyed. And this is dependent upon you looking unto God and determining in your heart that you wanted the more of him. Are you ready for your comeback?

10.

He kept me, just to make me

.......he hath sent me to bind up the brokenhearted, to proclaim liberty to the captives, and the opening of the prison to them that are bound;

Isaiah 61:1(partial)

I know that you have heard it said before that much of the trouble that we face in this life is birthed in the camp of the enemy. Much of the trouble that we are facing is because the enemy understands where God is getting ready to take us. He knows *the plans that God has for us, the plans to prosper us and give us an expected end.* The devil is forming weapons. He is building roadblocks. He is throwing traps in our way. He is tossing mind-disrupting grenades so as to bring to our remembrance the strongholds that once held us. All in an attempt to confine our thought life, if not totally undermine our physical or mental well being. The devil works to confound you. But the Bible reminds us that *the Lord shall deliver us from every evil work.* What the devil meant for evil God will turn it around for your eventual good. The scriptures also tell us that we who are in Christ are free.

For whatsoever is born of God overcometh the world: and this is the victory that overcometh the world, even our flesh. Who is he that overcometh the world, but he that believeth that Jesus is the Son of God.

1 John 5: 4,5

99

There's something about the awesomeness of the word of God. We are reminded throughout its pages of the faithfulness of God in saving us when we are in a time of trouble. Victory scriptures or deliverance scriptures are always easy to find. It's always easy to be encouraged by the fact that God has made a way out. But what if a way out is not the best idea? What do we do when the plan of God is not immediate relief? What if the plan of God for your life requires that you suffer for a little while?

How many of you are really and truly concerned about manifesting God's kingdom here on earth? In the Lord's prayer, Jesus directed us to beseech God that his kingdom may be established here on earth as it is in heaven. However, the bible warns us that we must through much tribulation enter into the kingdom of God. If God talks about trouble, trial and tribulation with such frequency and with such vivid detail why do we still believe that in salvation, God owes us an exemption from the trouble he promised.

As a child of God we must properly contend with the possibility that our life may involve a series or a season of confinement. How do I deal with the understanding that the trouble, and the constraint that I am experiencing may be a part of the providential will of God for my life? As we examine confinement and we juggle with the prospect of coping with it we must first get a clear understanding of God's intention for his people. We have to begin to ask some hard questions, some questions that have over the years been answered in myriad of ways. Questions like, are confinement and captivity and other such tactics part of God's plan? Does God subject his people to captivity and confinement? Does a just God allow his people to be constrained by an unjust world?

In the book of Daniel the prophet, we are introduced to a man of conviction. Actually he was quite a young man when we are given an account of who he is in the book that

Broken, *just to be made new*

is penned by him. Daniel is a teenager captured and taken exile to Babylon after the overthrow and the sacking of Jerusalem by the Persians. The Bible says that it was the third year of the reign of King Jehoiakim of Judah when the Babylonian king Nebuchadnezzar came to defeat, and to besiege Jerusalem. And the bible continues to say that the Lord gave the King of Judah over to the hands of the Babylonians. The Lord did not hand his people over to Babylon in the simple sense of the word but He did allow his people to fall captive to the Babylonians. If we study closely what had befallen the people of Israel one is made aware of the fact that they were in the age of apostasy. They had turned their backs on God. They had attached themselves to pagan Gods. They had intermarried with pagan men and women. Basically they had transgressed the law of God, broke their covenant, and as a result God had taken his hedge of protection away.

Most of the time the confinement that we find ourselves in is God allowed due to our transgression. We get confined to abusive marriages because we turned a deaf ear to the warning of God. We are confined to dead end jobs because we did not listen to God. We were selfish in our giving. We stole God's tithes. We paid some weeks but on the other weeks we bought a suit here and a pair of shoes there. We get confined to prison cells because we broke the commandments and stole, lied and killed. We get confined to a mindset of poverty because we live under a God ordained curse. We know that when we do wrong we become subject to the net that confines. But what if we did no apparent wrong and we are still confined. What if your confinement is as a result of your inheritance?

What if you were brought into captivity simply because of your birthright? This is no longer is a punitive confinement but rather is a restorative act of God. When you find yourself confined as a result of no direct fault of your own understand that God is up to something. When you find yourself trapped; ensnared by a divine act of God just stand. Daniel's confinement in this foreign land as a part of God's plan was not for his benefit alone. It was for God to get the glory. The life that Daniel lived in captivity, and under persecution, would live on as a testimony to God's faithfulness to those who stay faithful to Him.

In the midst of your brokenness and God ordained pain, when you can come to understand you were somebody before the confinement, you are somebody during the confinement and you will be somebody after the confinement victory is already yours. Daniel was described as being of the certain children of Israel that were of the king's seed and of the princes. Therefore that means that Daniel was royalty. His condition was one of captivity but his position was still one of royalty. The first tactic for surviving confinement is to know that confinement affects your condition and not your position. Daniel entered his captivity knowing that he was royalty. How many of you understand that despite the confining nature of our present circumstances in the eyes of God you are royalty?

He hath made us kings and priests unto God and His Father.
Revelation 1:6

But ye are a chosen generation, a royal priesthood, an holy nation.
1 Peter 2:9

Knowing that despite your physical state, despite societies labels placed upon you, you are a son of God makes you that much more prepared to deal with temporary setback and prepared to taste permanent victory.

There is a lesson to be learned in the limitations that God has placed on our lives. Recognition of and survival of brokenness is dependent on us knowing our limitations. The physicality's of life can be confining—as a three-dimensional being space and time confine us. Although my mind may wonder far beyond the walls of my prison, my physical body is restricted to the place on which I stand at any given moment in time. The Bible teaches us that we are spirit beings housed, or confined to a physical body. And our spirit is confined to the physical limits of our body. We have to know our limitations. In knowing our limitations we many times come to a better knowledge of ourselves.

Surviving the broken place is dependent also upon our harnessing of the strength in the struggle. The struggle, the discomfort, the uneasiness that develops in us, in our broken season despite the seeming damage it causes also can be a source of strength. When we are broken we appreciate and realize that we have confinements. We have confinements when it comes to lack of finances, less than desirable living conditions, limited education, low-income employment or even the physical bars of a real prison. We must realize that God is using this captivity, this season as a mode of preparation. God wants some of us to pray until something happens. This prayer might not move the bars, it might not shake the foundations of the prison but it should strengthen the foundations of your faith.

When I think of the strength hidden in the constraints that God may put on our lives I am reminded of weight training, and working out in the gym. We enter the gym in the early spring and in our minds we have some great expectations of how we will look by mid-summer. We come with a hope of developing our muscle, some of us go to the gym with an intent of losing weight and trimming down, others of us go to the gym actually looking to gain muscle mass. Each of us came into the gym with different pictures in our mind of what we would look like in just a few months. We have different goals but oddly enough we use much of the same tactics to achieve these goals. We get on the treadmill, we might even use the stationary bike, and we tackle the free-weights. We do each of these exercises in an effort to exert some pressure, tension and stress on our muscles.

Our muscles are confined to our physical flesh and the only way that we can expand them is to apply pressure, tension and stress through exercise. As we lose needless fat, we gain useful muscle and strength. When we workout, oxygen is driven into our lungs. As this oxygen is combined with glucose (i.e. simple sugar) and this mixture produces ATP (what we know as energy). This energy gives us the power to do work. It allows us to push harder, ride faster, and run longer. The faster the oxygen and sugar are combined at the cellular level the better. The confinement that is created as my muscles push against my skin creates strength. Confinement exerts not only physical stress but also spiritual stress. God desires to exercise our spiritual muscles, so that we might develop our spiritual strength.

11.

The Final Word

The hardest battle is to be oneself in a world that is doing its best to make you like everyone else.

E.F. Cummings

Human life is the condition of trying to conform to the molding of God while trying to resist the desire to fulfill the urges of your flesh. The spirit of man is earnestly opposing the soul of man but unfortunately man chooses to empower the soul, and neglect the spirit. Our soul can only express itself in one of three ways, "I want, I feel, or I think." And these are the very areas or expressions that initiate our downfall. When we become enslaved to what we want, what we feel, and what we think, we become independent of God. The devil's greatest victory over mankind was in suggesting to mankind that there was such a thing as independence.

> *Ye shall not surely die:*
> *For God doth know that in the day ye eat thereof, then your eyes shall be opened, and ye shall be as gods, knowing good and evil.*
>
> **Genesis 3:4b-5**

The serpent in essence told Eve that if she ate of the tree of knowledge, in direct disobedience to God's command, then she would position herself in such a way that she would no longer need to depend on God because she would become a god herself. The devil had her *feeling* that independence from God was better than dependence on an all-powerful Lord. And unfortunately, the enemy of our souls is still telling the same lie. He is still stoking the same feelings and emotions even today especially among unbelievers but even with professed believers too.

What we want, what we think and what we feel are the sole motivations for human behavior in the heart of one that has not had an encounter with God's abundant grace. These three motivations as innocent as they may appear can be fatal to the human life. In God's love for us we are many times thrust into the experience of brokenness. Brokenness is painful, uncomfortable and also can be humiliating. These are all adjectives that carry a negative connotation. As a result, our minds find it hard to equate the allowance of the experience to the act of a gracious and loving God. Our minds clouded by the misconceptions pervading in popular culture like; just do it, and if it feels good try it, and you have to worry only about yourself, and as long as you are okay with it do it; we see no value in persecution, trial and trouble that comes with breaking.

The devil will have us to believe that persecution is an indication that we are outside of the will of God. His greatest strategy is to have us to believe that God is our enemy. If He's a loving God why would he put you through such hardship? That is the question that he asks us today. We must understand that the easiest way to forge an alliance is for us to create a common enemy between us. This is the mindset that the devil uses in his dealing with us, and in his attempt to make us misinterpret the purpose behind our trials. The breaking, as defined in all of the previous chapters, believe it or not, is designed to bring our wants, feelings and thoughts under the control of the Spirit of God.

Broken, *just to be made new*

Trouble may come, trials may even persist but God spoke a divine promise over your life. When he uttered, "Weeping may endure for a night, but joy comes in the morning," he was speaking to you. Despair may set up camp in your situation, causing a shadow of doubt to cloud your mind. You have to tell yourself that doubt and despair are just squatters. They are illegally residing on the private property of your mind because God has made you a promise.

It's promised that you will have joy. It's promised that you shall overcome. It's promised that we shall win in the end. Any attack that you might be experiencing today is just that an attack. One attack does not a battle make. One attack is not a victory won. Attack does not mean defeat. Things lost does not mean forever unreturned. Dreams dashed do not mean death because my ordained destiny speaks louder than any defiant speech of the enemy. He speaks defeat in one ear but God shouts victory in my heart.

My mind understands the reality of failure but my heart knows the truth of favor. With every setback, I take a step back and look at where God has brought me from and I understand that I am a threat to the enemy's schemes. If I keep walking away from the former things then all those connected to me will follow; and this will upset the enemy's plan to steal, kill and destroy. Every look I take into my past confirms and affirms that my breakthrough is just about to come to pass. I'm that much closer.

The hardest thing for us to do is praise God in the midst of the struggle. It seems antithetical to even conjure up a level of joyous reverence to God when all that we are feeling is hurt and pain. However, as we advance we must give God praise. Even in our *go through* we must worship. The fact that we are going through tells us that it's not a permanent situation. It reminds us that the circumstance that we may find ourselves in; that which gives us a sense of dis-ease is really just a temporary location, and a moment in time. It is a temporary place, a season in time and a mitigating circumstance that shall never be the same again.

God meant it to be so. He meant it to be so that we might learn patience. The apostle James beseeched the people of God to let patience have her perfect work. When we let patience work into our lives we become perfect and we mature and become the complete men and women that God is calling us to be. God meant it for you to be tested so that you might grow in your faith. The scripture reminds us that the trying of our faith *worketh* patience. That means that the exercising of faith is an act of activating patience.

When our faith is tried we can look at it from one of two positions. We can assert that we are standing in a place of empowerment through the development of patience in us or we can look at it as an attempt to make us fall therefore deeming it a temptation. But we must understand that this temptation is not a scheme designed to trip you but rather is an act purposed to test your faith. This is where we get confused many times in God's dealing with us. We lump temptation and test all into the same bag. In our minds both of them are meant to trap or trick you. Temptations rightly so should be seen as a trap but tests are not. They are mechanisms by which we can evaluate our strengths and our weaknesses. Tests are evaluating tools and this is how God uses them to prove our faithfulness toward Him.

These tests are events in our walk of faith that cause us to pull on the reins of that faith. These are the things that make us question ourselves. They cause us to re-evaluate the motives behind what we do, say or even think. God is not the one on trial here, or His Word. But rather, it is you. You are on trial when today's events impose on your yesterday faith and call it to become, "now faith." This is the type of faith that gives me the confidence to believe that I already have the house of my dreams, the spouse of my

dreams, the car of my dreams, and the ministry of my
dreams even if I can't see it. I still know that I have it.

As you contemplate your brokenness, or as you think
about the breaking of your past I implore you to
acknowledge this fact. In the kingdom of God the only valid
currency is faith. It comes in several denominations because
God said that he gives to all a measure of faith according to
ones abilities. Even though your faith may seem miniscule
compared to your friend just remember that even your little
has legal access to the Father. The only legal tender
accepted in the spirit realm is faith. Fear is a counterfeit
replication of faith that possesses the same capabilities in
the carnal man that faith has in the righteous. Fear is the
materializing or the substantiating of all that negatively
lurked in your mind. Fear has the same power as faith to
create in our minds reality that has not yet been realized.
Lay fear aside and hold fast to faith or else you will
unconsciously attract defeat into our lives.

Faith is the substance that creates a conviction in us
for the things we desire through God. In our season of
brokenness our safest retreat is into the arms of our faith in
God. Abel died a physical death at the hands of a vengeful
brother but his act of faithful sacrifice allowed his spirit to
live on vicariously before God. Faith is powerful and
sustaining. It is intimately related to favor. Favor
unattached from faith is short-lived and seasonal, while
favor wrapped in faith is continuously accessible to us.

To truly understand our season of brokenness we
must have a heart transformation. Our hearts must be
made conscious of the spirit of God that Christ made
available to us. Our hearts must be introduced to the
comforter. However, as long as we walk according to our
carnal desires the Spirit of the Lord desiring to make an
impression in your life will be placed in a realm of conflict.
As long as we walk by the way that gives us the greatest joy

in the physical, and the greatest high in the natural, the potential for our spirit to grow in the strength of God is stifled.

The problem is my heart.

And God saw that the wickedness of man was great in the earth, and that every imagination of the thoughts of his heart was only evil continually.

Genesis 6:5

The thoughts of our heart can be the main thing that gets us off the right track. We follow our heart's desires but many times our hearts are pointing in the wrong direction. God said that David had a heart that was after God. It wasn't that David did no wrong but rather it was that his heart kept a constant vigil and search after the things of God. He desired to please God. Even after an act of sin he sought ways to commend his sin unto God. He did not so much wonder about his actions effects on men, but rather he focused on making things right with God.

Friend, I ask you today as you have come to the end of this exposition, as I descend from my soap box and I take my place next to you, as we stand before God, broken; where do we go from here? There are always options. There is never just one way to go. Peter, the chief apostle, Jesus' enforcer stood right where we stand. When I opened this book I said that he was broken too. Did that brokenness take away from what God had ordained over his life? Did that brokenness exclude him from the promise? After he went back to being a fisherman in the sea of Galilee, the very place that Jesus had taken him from to follow him, did God just forget about him? My friend, no, He didn't. All that Peter did still didn't cancel the promise that God made to him. This is why I stand here with you now, before the throne of grace and the seat of mercy and I proclaim that if God said it, I've got to believe it and I'm coming out the

Broken, just to be made new

better for it even after this. I encourage you to follow me in that declaration and watch God make you new once more.

Hugh J Harmon

Broken,
just to be made new
Life Experience Journal

Overcoming the feeling of failure in your life

"Life has a way of sometimes handing us outcomes that fall way short of our expectations. Disappointment can many times be the daunting companion of great expectations. The frequency with which we encounter short falls can cause us to adopt an attitude of failure."
                                                    -Hugh Harmon

1. Have you ever felt like a failure? Describe the situation and how you handled it. _____

_____

_____

_____

_____

_____

2. What is your definition of failure? Has it changed over the years? Why or why not?

_____

_____

_____

_____

_____

_____

_____

_____

3. List some things that you believe you failed at completing in the past due to your initial lack of preparedness. For each endeavor listed think about the reasons why you failed.

_____

_____

_____

_____

_____

_____

_____

_____

_____

_____

_____

4. What are some of the things that you failed at in the past but today you are now better equipped to be a success in them?

_____

_____

_____

_____

_____

_____

_____

_____

_____

_____

_____

_____

Now make a plan, and go after it!

Becoming Undone

"For many of us being broken is not as impending as Marsha's bout with a bruised self-esteem. Sometimes the episode of breaking can be totally unexpected—one moment on top of the world, the other desiring to be under it."
-Hugh Harmon

1. Describe a time when you were faced with some of the experiences or feelings described in *Becoming Undone*.
   _____
   _____
   _____
   _____
   _____
   _____
   _____

2. In your personal experience of *Becoming Undone* was it a sudden breakdown or a gradual loss of control? Was there anything that you can now look at in hindsight and say with certainty that it should have been an indicator of trouble? _____
   _____
   _____
   _____
   _____

3. How would you describe what it means to worship?
   _____
   _____
   _____
   _____
   _____
   _____

4. What are some things that you are waiting on God to do for you?

_____

_____

_____

The Blessing in Brokenness

"There is no prerequisite of salvation or spiritual rebirth in order for one to be entangled in brokenness. But there is a spiritual requirement for one to come out on the other side of it all, better off than when you entered in."
-Hugh Harmon

1. Have you ever been in a predicament or a crisis in which you learned a great lesson? What was the predicament and what was the lesson?

   _____
   _____
   _____
   _____
   _____
   _____

2. What advise would you give to a friend or a family member that is going through a rough season?

   _____
   _____
   _____
   _____
   _____

3. Think of the opportunities that you had this week to minister to someone even in the midst of a struggle about the goodness of God toward you in your time of struggle. How would you explain to them about God's purpose behind it all?

   _____
   _____
   _____
   _____

Pained for a Purpose

"Brokenness becomes necessary for us when our view of God and our relationship to Him is based on our knowledge and experience of the natural relationships of our past."

-Hugh Harmon

1. What would you say are the greatest challenges to your faith in God thus far?

_____

_____

_____

_____

_____

_____

2. How was your relationship to your father growing up, and how is it now?

_____

_____

_____

_____

_____

_____

3. Are there any issues that you faced with your father that you find yourself confronting with God?

_____

_____

_____

_____

_____

_____

4. Go to the book of Exodus and read about the experience of Moses up until his calling to lead the people out of Egypt. What were some of his experiences with the father figures in his life? What lesson can you learn from it?

_____

_____

_____

_____

_____

_____

Strong in the broken places

"Before God can use me, He must first make me useful."

-Hugh Harmon

1. Have you ever gained strength from a bad situation? How were you able to do it?

_____

_____

_____

_____

_____

_____

2. What was it that set the woman with an issue of blood apart from all the other sick and infirmed people in the crowd that surrounded Jesus

_____

_____

_____

_____

_____

_____

3. For the next two weeks every time you encounter bad news or a challenging circumstance I want you to take inventory and list all the possible positive outcomes that you can from the entire situation.

_____

_____

_____

_____

_____

_____

4. Study the tragedy of Samson. How was his broken place experience actually changed into a monumental occasion of gathering strength when all the odds were turned against him?

_____

_____

_____

_____

_____

_____

_____

Growing Pains

"Pain that is present keeps me seeking a remedy.
While pain that is past informs me that I'm healed."
-Hugh Harmon

1. What changes have you experienced in your life that mark a degree of growth on your part?

_____
_____
_____
_____
_____
_____

2. How were those changes painful for you to do? What about those changes was painful?

_____
_____
_____
_____
_____
_____

3. Inevitably we all need to continue to grow in certain areas of our life. In what areas do you still see growth potential? How will that growth impact your life and your relationships?

_____
_____
_____
_____
_____
_____

4. I've found that creating an acronym for certain principles has made those principles a concrete part of my conscious memory. What acronym can you create for the word, GROW using the precepts discussed in this chapter?

G- _____

R- _____

O- _____

W- _____

Ready to die

"When we starve our souls of the emotional triggers that once bathed our consciences we actually deal a deathblow to our will. This death is our breaking. Are you willing to break away from that old habit?"

-Hugh Harmon

1. What are the things that you are ready to die for?

_____
_____
_____
_____
_____
_____

2. From the list of things that you are ready to die for did you list anything that was detrimental to your general welfare?

_____
_____
_____
_____
_____
_____

3. Peter proclaimed in one of his moments of exclamation without contemplation that he was ready to die for Christ. However, when he was asked if he had been one of Christ's followers he denied even knowing who Jesus was. He succumbed to fear. Have you ever fallen into the trap of fear? How will you deal with challenges to your faith?

_____
_____
_____
_____

You're not your own

"There is no place that we could go that will render us far enough away from God to make his influence in our lives limited."

-Hugh Harmon

1. How would you rate your level of independence in life from the influence or assistance of others? Why?

_____
_____
_____
_____
_____
_____

3. Who are the people in your life that you depend on for your survival, indirectly or directly? Why?

_____
_____
_____
_____
_____
_____
_____

4. How would you communicate to a friend or an associate about the necessity for them to develop a dependency on God for guidance and protection? How do you ensure that you are depending on God's guidance and protection in your own life?

5. _____
_____
_____
_____
_____
_____
_____

Hugh J Harmon

You're not forgotten

"As a human being existing in a fallen world our lives are betwixt and between a paradigm. The enemy of our soul is out to get rid of us, and God is out to restore us."
-Hugh Harmon

1. When was the last time you were a blessing to someone else?

_____
_____
_____
_____
_____
_____

2. In your opinion, how does blessing others affect your storehouse?

_____
_____
_____
_____
_____
_____

3. In what areas of your life do you sometimes feel that God has forgotten you in?

_____
_____
_____
_____
_____
_____

4. Think about different ways that you can help others through their pain and in doing so help yourself through yours. When you don't forget others, God won't forget you.

_____

_____

_____

_____

_____

_____

He kept me, just to make me

"In the midst of your brokenness and God ordained pain, when you can come to understand you were somebody before the confinement, you are somebody during the confinement, and you will be somebody after the confinement; victory is already yours."
                                        -Hugh Harmon

1. At what point in your go-through did you decide to give it over to God? Explain.

_____

_____

_____

_____

_____

_____

2. Can you think of any difficult circumstances under which you found yourself that actually confirmed that God might be up to something in your life?

_____

_____

_____

_____

_____

3. What advice would you give to someone who has been through a similar stint of difficulty as yours and may be losing faith in God to deliver them?

_____

_____

_____

_____

_____

If this book has been a blessing to you, we would love you to give us some feedback. *"Great opportunities to do goodwill are few and far between, but small moments to make a difference through God's will are ever before us."* And my desire through each and every book that I write is to not only leave an impression but more significantly to make an impact. Take some time to reflect on how this book has affected the way that you saw yourself or the way that you saw others. Send your correspondence to Hugh J. Harmon., **Blessedhugh2@aol.com** and **PastorHugh@lovefellowshipkingdomrestorationtabernacle.org**

Or log onto Hugh J. Harmon's myspace page.
www.myspace.com/fromrebel2righteousness
and our ministry page
www.myspace.com/lftkingdomrestoration
And leave a blog comment.

Or send us mail...
Hugh J. Harmon
Kingdom Book & Gift LLP
PO Box 291975
Columbia, SC 29229